LOW-CARB
ITALIAN
COOKING
with The Love Chef

OTHER BOOKS BY FRANCIS ANTHONY

Cooking Pasta with Love

Cooking with Love, Italian Style

Cooking with Love: The Love Chef Shows You How

LOW-CARB
ITALIAN
COOKING

with *The Love Chef*

Delicious Italian Recipes for
Today's New Lifestyle

The Love Chef
FRANCIS ANTHONY

M. Evans & Company, Inc.
New York

M. Evans and Company, Inc.
216 East 49th Street
New York, NY 10017

Book design and type formatting by Bernard Schleifer
Manaufactured in the United States of America

In loving memory of my
Mom and Dad

Contents

In the Beginning

I FIRST MET Dr. Robert Atkins several years ago when we were guests on a popular radio talk show. He with his *Atkins Diet Revolution* book and me with my *Pasta* book—talk about the odd couple!

What a charged program; chatting between commercials, he suggested to me that it is easy to maintain a healthy low-carb way of eating, even with Italian food. "Start by taking the pasta out," he said. "Your Italian recipes will work on a low-carb diet plan." Well over forty years ago, Dr. Atkins started to promote his low-carb, high-fat diet. Today the Atkins diet has gained the stamp of approval from the medical community.

Well, thank you, Dr. Atkins. Low-carb Italian-style cooking is here. I don't adhere strictly to the Atkins philosophy—I advocate low carbs (not no carbs) and I'm not a fan of high fat—I walk the middle of the road. These recipes represent what I feel is a healthy way of eating: high in taste, low-to-moderate carbs, and low in fat. Everything in moderation.

Whether or not you are on a diet, this book should please you. By manipulating a few subtle ingredients, I give you the results your body wants and the taste your mouth savors. *Mangia!*

Why This Book?

*P*LAIN AND SIMPLE—we need to incorporate into our diet easy-to-prepare, satisfying food that helps you to shed unwarranted, unhealthy pounds and/or maintain an ideal weight. If you are a diabetic, then you'll benefit from the low carb counts in these delicious recipes.

THIS BOOK CAN HELP!

I've matched the low-carb foods you like with great healthy results—you can enjoy eating everyday. I lost thirty pounds and fifteen points of bad cholesterol; mind you, this is while I "ate" my way through twenty-two Italian cities, twelve Australian/New Zealand cities, and over seventy-five American cities. Even I was amazed; it is so simple eating these recipes with low carbs—*low carbs*!

THIS BOOK CAN HELP

Obesity has reached an all-time epidemic level. We're a gorge-yourself, supersize-it, high-carb society. Children are the real losers, affected by additional weight early on and developing a pattern of poor eating habits that is compounded daily.

THIS BOOK CAN HELP

Obesity has taken its toll:

Diabetes	Premature death
Asthma	Coronary heart disease
High blood pressure	Rheumatoid arthritis
Birth defects	Breast and other cancers
Cardiovascular disease	Carpel tunnel syndrome
Deep vein thrombosis	Daytime sleepiness
Gall bladder disease	Infertility
Liver disease	Low back pain
Gout	Surgical complications
Stroke	Urinary stress incontinence
Sleep apnea	Impaired immune response

THIS BOOK CAN HELP

You'll be eating great-tasting food that is healthy, but I'm not calling it "health food." I'll get you on the road to enjoying food and tasting and creating other recipes on your own.

All this carb talk, what is a carb? Short for . . .

CARBOHYDRATE

Carb refers to carbon

Hydrate refers to water

A combination of carbon, hydrogen, and oxygen, carbs are plants' own food source.

Carbs are *one* of three major groups of nutrients that provide *calories*. The other two are protein and fat. They provide energy, vitamins, minerals, fiber, and phytochemicals that fuel our muscles and brain and provide our heartbeat. Each gram of carbohydrate provides four calories of energy.

Fats and *meats* do not contain carbs. Everything else has carbs.

The *simplest carbs*, like sugar (glucose) and refined white flour, are the quickest to digest, hence the insulin spike they produce in the body, and their more rapid storage as fat.

Complex carbs, such as those found in whole grains and fruits and vegetables, take longer to digest.

Okay, so why do we gain weight from eating carbs?

The answer is simple: if the carbs are not burned off, they'll be stored as fat! Realize that, although *simple carbs* can give you a quick boost in energy, blood sugar levels drop quickly, and you will feel tired and lethargic. If those extra carbs are not burned, *here comes that fat.*

Complex carbs convert to glycogen and are released slowly into the muscles throughout your body and the liver and are stored until required, but once the body's glycogen needs are met, *excess* complex carbs will also be stored as fat!

WE HAVE TO STOP THE INSANITY

Reduce or eliminate foods containing refined flour and/or refined sugar, such as soda, cookies, cakes, candy, desserts, and sugar-filled cereals. Incorporate more fiber, whole grains, and other complex carbs in your diet.

THIS BOOK CAN HELP

If you just cook these recipes, eat the recommended portion, and watch your intake of those foods containing refined flour and sugar, *you will lose weight.*

Introduction

$\mathscr{M}$Y LOVE AFFAIR with food, cooking, and people begain many years ago. I was six years old when I asked to become involved in creating delicious entrees, tasty side dishes, and delectable desserts. My earliest memories bring back the smell of the family kitchen, with sauces simmering and meat roasting.

I can also recall the sounds of the kitchen—the chopping of vegetables, the sizzling of fried foods, the conversation and laughter around the table. My love of cooking and entertaining was reinforced by preparing and sharing wonderful meals with relatives and friends. What a great combination! Today, that love affair is still going strong, so it's appropriate that I'm known as "The Love Chef."

How can you be a Love Chef, too? It's simple! Enjoy what you're doing. Have fun. Make mistakes. Try again. Take the time to appreciate the textures, colors, shapes, and smells. Squeeze plump red tomatoes between your fingers, toss crisp salad greens with your hands, feel the grainy spices.

Appreciating the special qualities of foods will enhance the cooking experience. Get to know familiar and new foods. Soon, produce and meats will become less confusing and more inspiring.

Cooking with love goes beyond the act of cooking itself. It's entertaining with love as well. One of the greatest benefits of cooking wonderful meals is sharing them with the people you love. Regardless of what you prepare, serve it with style. Light a few candles. Use place cards. Get out the best china. Set the table with love!

I've taught for years using this philosophy, and it's gratifying to see the results. People always tell me that the lessons they learn extend well beyond the kitchen. Their experience leads to a stronger love of life!

Spreading my passion for the culinary arts, I've been able to educate people about food preparation and serving techniques in a number of ways. As founder of The Cooking with Love School, I led a comprehensive program for men and women, which included instructors from around the world. My "Little Chefs" program inspired children to become a part of mealtime preparation as well, giving them practical skills and well-earned pride in their accomplishments.

With the experience of running a successful school, I turned to other venues to attract would-be chefs. Using department store and supermarket venues, I initiated smaller cooking classes, during which enrollees could learn basic skills or enhance the ability they had.

My unique approach prompted *Time* magazine to report that I "had a handle on the coming food explosion!" And what an explosion it is! Interest in cooking and entertaining continues to grow, and I'm thrilled to be a part of it.

Today the love for food is being adapted to incorporate a love of your body. Healthful, yet satisfying, meals are on everyone's wish list. More often than not, I am given the challenge of creating menus that will please the senses, nourish the body, and respect dietary needs. Always one to stay on top of the latest trends, I am pleased to bring you this collection of low-carb Italian recipes—the best of both worlds!

Recipes in this book have the same high quality you've come to trust from my television and stage appearances. Throughout my twenty years as a regular on *Live with Regis and Kelly* (formerly *Live with Regis and Kathie Lee*), I've earned your trust as a resource for great-tasting recipes, and I know you'll agree that this book is as exciting as my previous three.

More recipes, as well as other helpful information, may be found pn my Web site, www.thelovechef.com. We've got a special section just for kids so they can join the fun, too!

Grab a wooden spoon and your favorite saucepan as we venture into the new and improved world of healthy, low-carb, restaurant-quality Italian food. And you'll fall in love, too!

Buon appetito!
Your Love Chef

Presentation

BEFORE GETTING TO the recipes, I want to talk about ambience. Ambience is an important a part of the dining experience as the food you eat, because the sights and sounds and feelings around your table contribute equally to making dinner just what you want it to be—calm and restful, romantic and exciting, or giddy and fun. Even before you turn on the oven, turn on the eyes. Present your meal as attractively as you can. Here's what I like to see on a dinner table.

Plain white or soft beige dishes for your one basic set, nothing can beat plain white or soft beige dishes. They create the most handsome background for your foods and, depending on the rest of the table setting, can look informal or elegant. Keep the plates simple and let the food itself be your design. If you are someone who enjoys shopping for dinnerware and your budget can handle it, it's fun to have a variety of place settings for two—maybe bright country style, maybe rustic brown plates. Don't let your good china collect dust on an inaccessible shelf in the cupboard. Keep two place settings down on the easy-to-reach shelves and bring them out to use now and then to give your spirits a lift.

Linen napkins. If you have some of those old-fashioned, oversized linen napkins that your grandmother gave you, use them for special dinners for two. There is something about a very big, very soft white linen dinner napkin that makes any meal seem classy. But always use cloth napkins! Buy cotton ones in a variety of colors and vary them with the seasons or to suit your table setting or mood. Cloth napkins are infinitely nicer than paper, and they're easy to wash.

White candles (lots of them) add a special feeling to any meal. I like both tall ones in candle holders and the short, stubby kind that sit in low glass containers and can be massed around for a dramatic effect. Don't make the mistake of thinking candles are for dressy occasions only; candles are for every day.

Placemats. Here is another inexpensive and easy way to give a table a little style and polish. Simple straw mats look great on butcher-block kitchen tables; mirrored glass mats look really special for a command performance dinner.

Flowers. I love them on a dinner table, or anywhere! Put a big bunch of daisies in a chunky earthenware pot. Put a single iris or daffodil in a clear, thin vase. Buy some potted geraniums and put them on the table or around the area where you'll be eating.

Flowers and greens look great hooked on a pegboard or on adjacent counters. The centerpiece doesn't have to be flowers at all. A bunch of gourds, small melons, or dried artichokes sitting right on the table or in straw baskets gives a bright, cheery look to any meal.

Candlelight, a pretty and colorful table, fresh flowers—all these are a way of saying *I love you*, a way of treating the eye as well as the taste buds, of making a meal an entertainment.

Your eating environment. You don't *have* to eat at the official dining table—be creative. Maybe the evening you are planning suggests buffet-style dishes served up in the kitchen, or plates brought out to a low coffee table in front of the living-room couch for cozy and casual ambience. Maybe your guest is a football freak and you're planning a Monday-night-in-front-of-the-TV kind of dinner. Then you might set up trays or small tables in the TV room, or clear the desk. Another nice dinner might utilize an electric wok—a wonderful appliance that's not at all hard to use—bring it into the bedroom or out on your terrace. Look around your space with an open mind and don't be afraid to think in terms of a movable feast.

Couples need special loving care at night. Let dinner be a time to relax, unwind, and switch from the mental pressures of a busy day to the sensual delights of dinner for two. Disconnect the phone, light a candle or two, leave a love note under your mate's dinner plate, and design a meal to fit the day. If one partner had a heavy business lunch, then it's time for a light and easy dinner, maybe a seafood salad or shrimp in red bell pepper sauce. If your partner has been traveling and is getting back home for the first time in a day or two or more, it's time to plan something slow and elegant. If you have kids, this type of romantic meal may not be so easy to enjoy, so plan for it—send the kids to a movie with the sitter or to a friend's house for a sleepover, but take the time to enjoy a pleasant meal.

Of course, dining as a family at the table and not in front of the TV is also important to teach children, to help develop their eating patterns and table manners.

It also allows a family to communicate and discuss their day's activities. It's unfortunate that many families dine in their cars at the drive-thru.

A WORD ABOUT MENU PLANNING

A well-planned meal should be orchestrated, not contrived. Decide first on a main course and let your complementary courses build on it. The entree is the focal point and usually the heartiest or most substantial part of the meal, and its taste should dominate. Keep soups or other first courses lighter than the entree and think of accompanying vegetables in terms of how attractive they will look, as well as how well they will complement the centerpiece dish. Remember your total carb count. Avoid one-color meals and meals composed of elements that are all soft and mushy or hard and crunchy. Strive for balance, variety, and interest.

As I say over and over, a cookbook isn't a Bible, it's just a guide to look to for suggestions and ideas, information, and inspiration. Use cookbooks as your guides and then adapt the recipes to suit your tastes and needs. Ten people cooking the same recipe will turn out ten different dishes, each taking on a little of the personality of the cook creating it and varying with the quality of the ingredients, the way your particular oven works, et cetera. The same holds true for planning a meal.

THE "ITALIAN" KITCHEN SETUP

Your kitchen should be a comfy work center that will make you happy. Bring in a television or radio so you can watch or listen to your favorite show or tape; fill the walls with framed posters, pictures, and love letters; have a cordless phone. Don't hide pots and pans on high shelves; hang them or keep them in bottom cabinets. Pegboards and hooks work wonders even in the smallest galley kitchens. The more equipment you have out and available, the easier it will be to cook and the more fun you will have doing it.

Shelves of attractive glass or plastic canisters filled with herbs, spices, pasta of many shapes, and other dry foods give an uncluttered look and are ready and at hand when something is needed quickly. Also, the different shapes and textures of the food create an attractive appearance.

An added benefit for a wall display is the space it will leave you in your cabinets. Store those items not often used, such as large platters, large mixing bowls, baking pans, and other odd-sized items. Dishes, glassware, condiments, and grocery goods should be convenient.

The lighting should be comfortable. I love dimmers in the kitchen to change the mood; a soft light is so much more appealing than a glaring bright one. A counter light over your work area is also very important.

If you have a large kitchen, a good work center is a must. It will quickly turn into a talk center, a quick-bite center, a drying-tears center, and a chatting-on-the-phone center.

Even a smaller kitchen should have a rolling butcher block or table that can be used for other things. Throw a tablecloth over it and it becomes a great serving cart, an extra table for parties, or a dinner table in front of the TV. It also makes a versatile buffet table and a convenient bar for parties; the bottom can hold tubs of ice and wine/beer and can be easily rolled from the kitchen into the "action" and back again for refilling. The top is great for liquor and fixings.

COOKWARE

A good set of everyday cookware is a wise investment. Avoid dime-store-variety pots and pans. I prefer *heavy* stainless steel in a variety of sizes for ease in the cleanup process. The timing directions I give in the following recipes work for my pots. You may find a slight difference with your own cookware, so you should adjust times accordingly.

Of course, sharing the cleanup chores with someone is a blessing, and you can chat or watch TV at the same time.

NECESSARY TOOLS AND GADGETS

Everyone would like to have a fully equipped kitchen, but the primary tools you'll need to prepare your everyday meals are a knife, a plastic cutting board, wooden spoons, and a good set of cookware. It is great to have a food processor, but a basic kitchen can get along fine without one for everyday meals.

KNIVES

Choosing your basic chef's knife is one of your most important kitchen decisions. You can recognize a good (12 to 14-inch) chef's knife when you see that the blade continues into the handle and is embedded in it. Hold the knife in your hand; it should feel comfortable and well balanced. In addition to this basic knife, you will need slicing, carving, and paring knives, and a vegetable peeler.

FINDING THE TOOLS

Always remember when buying a particular utensil or gadget to look for durability and ease of cleaning. Sure, you'll collect all kinds of things, but buy what you'll really use from time to time to reduce your kitchen work. If you are near a town that has a restaurant-supply house, it would make sense to poke around and see what you can add to your collection. Flea markets and garage sales are good sources for everyday items as well as unusual serving pieces. When I was putting together my cooking school, I found dozens of unusual trays and serving pieces all in one afternoon at a large flea market in Edison, New Jersey.

Collect baskets to use as food holders; they make a great presentation. Baskets of different shapes and sizes create visual excitement and can be used for a variety of jobs. If you have the room, hang them in your kitchen.One Christmas, I had to pick up some visiting aunts at Radio City Music Hall in Manhattan. At the last minute, I grabbed one of my large baskets and lined it with red and green napkins. I threw in a couple of glass cups, apple-cinnamon shortbread cookies (they weren't into low-carb), and a large jar of my homemade eggnog.

I drove them all over the city to see the Christmas windows and lights of holiday New York as they enjoyed that snack. They had such a great time and are still talking about my "pretty basket" presentation.

CUTTING BOARDS

Wooden cutting boards have no place in my kitchen other than as trays or bread boards. Plastic cutting boards come in numerous sizes and can be easily sanitized, making bacteria less of a problem.

WOODEN SPOONS

I love wooden spoons, lots of them, in all sizes, because they are great for stirring and scraping. The one you've seen me use on television is Mom's, with the original crack from the time my brother said something she didn't like.

About the Recipes

$\mathscr{T}$HIS IS A COLLECTION of Italian recipes that are designed to be lower in carbs than usual.

So what can you expect? Be assured The Love Chef recipes' taste and quality remain as great as ever. This is the same great Italian food you want to serve your whole family. There's nothing mysterious about my recipes; sometimes I've substituted some ingredients with more traditional ones to reach our goal, but I guarantee that you either have the ingredients on your shelf or they are readily available. Here are some examples:

Soy flour. Soy flour is a major player in my low-carb Italian recipes, as it is used for dusting or dredging meat, fish, poultry, and vegetables. Universally recognized as healthier and lower in carbohydrates than white flour, soy flour is used to replace everyday white flour (with the exception of use as a thickening agent) in the recipes in this book. If you've never used soy flour before, don't be afraid. Soy imparts no taste of its own, so you'll be cutting carbs without losing familiar tastes. Soy flour is readily available in health food stores and is now appearing in supermarkets.

Parmigiano-Reggiano "breadcrumbs." Equal amounts of coarsely grated Parmigiano-Reggiano cheese mixed with an equal part of soy flour replaces breadcrumbs in recipes that call for them.

This combination is a delicious replacement for breadcrumbs. In fact, I like it so much I just may stop using breadcrumbs completely.

Pasta. Try as I might, I just cannot give up pasta completely. I know there are some new low-carb pastas or near pastas as well as ones made of soy on the supermarket shelves, but I prefer, and will not give up, my imported Italian pasta. My favorite brand is Colavita, which is made from the hardiest Italian semolina wheat from the fields of Molise.

I leave it for you to judge when and where you would accompany any of the recipes here with a small taste (2 ounces) of pasta (7 grams of protein, 30% thiamine, 15% niacin, 10% iron, 10% riboflavin and 30% folic acid). If you do, let me let you in on a secret: cook the pasta *al dente*, literally "to the tooth." Al dente pasta is chewy and slightly tougher than pasta that has been cooked thoroughly. By using this method, there is a lower glycemic level and, as a result, a slower conversion to sugar.

Olive Oil. Good Italian olive oil is a must when you cook my recipes. It has zero carbs, and it's a healthy monounsaturated fat. My absolute favorite, Colavita Extra Virgin Olive Oil, a true Italian olive oil produced and bottled in Italy, is a staple in all my kitchens, those in my schools and on TV.

During the olive oil harvest in the Molise region, my annual pilgrimage finds me with several lucky Colavita recipe contest winners (check my Web site for details).

Sugar/Sugar Substitutes. Sugar is 100 percent carbohydrate, pure and simple! So, we must eliminate it.

Unfortunately, on a daily basis, Americans consume an average of twenty teaspoons of sugar, which calculates to 110,000 calories a year. Sweetened beverages and desserts are the major culprits.

Whenever possible, I have substituted Splenda for sugar. Splenda, the trade name of a new dietary sweetener called sucralose, is pretty amazing stuff. It is not a chemical but is made from sugar that has been modified at the molecular level. As a result, Splenda tastes like sugar but has zero calories. Splenda Granular measures like sugar, has no unpleasant aftertaste, doesn't break down under high heat, and is safe for everyone (even kids) to eat. Since, other than sweetening, Splenda doesn't have the same properties as sugar, Splenda will not make a dish brown or a cake rise. So sometimes a small amount of sugar or other natural sweetener must be used in order for a recipe to have a palatable or aesthetic result. The added carbs are negligible.

Splenda comes both in individual packets—each packet sweetens like two teaspoons of sugar—and in granular form which measures like sugar, spoon for spoon. Bulking agents in Splenda Granular provide a minute amount of carbohydrate calories—six per tablespoon.

Milk. Where possible, I use heavy cream or half-and-half instead of milk for a lower carb count. However, in certain recipes, you may substitute whole or low-fat milk if you want a lower fat count and don't mind a few extra carbs.

PORTIONS

Serving size. Most of the main-course recipes, unless otherwise noted, serve four sensible portions. I've taken into consideration, as you should, the other courses you will have. Obviously, carbs, calories, etc., will be lower if you increase the number of servings, making the serving size smaller. I've added yield where appropriate to appetizers.

Typical size of products, unless otherwise noted in the recipe:

		Approxomite
Yellow onions	Small	6 ounces—Tennis ball
	Medium	8 ounces—Baseball
	Large	12 ounces—Softball
Eggplant	Medium	1 pound
	Large	1¾ pounds
Spinach	Since spinach is sold by bunches, prebagged, and loose, each recipe specifies weight.	

INGREDIENT CHOICES

Anchovies: I love anchovies and I know many people don't or think they don't. Anchovies are an ingredient in many sauces, and one I know you've used is Worcestershire sauce. In my recipes they are cooked and blended in to give the dish a particular taste. This differs from the "old" anchovies that were sitting on that slice of pizza you had years ago. I usually rinse them before using.

Artichokes: Fresh artichokes are usually readily available. When I use commercially packed artichokes, I opt for frozen, *not* vinaigretted. The ready-to-serve jarred marinated product is generally used for an appetizer platter.

Butter: Unsalted where we want the taste of butter but not additional salt.

Canned fruits: There are fewer carbs in *water*-packed canned fruits than in those packed in syrup and, the reason is obvious. But interestingly, one 2½-inch diameter fresh Bartlett pear contains about 25.1 carbs, while its water-packed canned equivalent has about 15.2 carbs. Although they may not be easy to find, check carbs on labels.

Canned tuna: If you've never tried canned *Italian* tuna fish packed in olive oil (zero carbs) you're missing a great treat. Not only can you just enjoy it as is, but it can become a quick meal with salads or veggies. Choose the lowest-carb veggies.

Chicken: Whole chicken breasts are usually found split (halved) in most markets. Each chicken recipe gives a portion size and states whether the chicken used should be boned, skinless, et cetera.

Chicken cutlet: The white meat flattened.

Chocolate: Good quality sugar-free chocolates are becoming readily available. You can also use grated unsweetened baker's chocolate, as I have in some recipes.

Eggplant: You can eliminate some of the bitterness by slicing the eggplant, salting the slices, and letting them drain in a colander for at least 30 minutes prior to cooking.

Eggs: Large.

Mushroom: Common white mushrooms (unless otherwise specified).

Pancetta: A cured Italian ham used similarly to bacon.

Parsley: Flat-leaf Italian variety.

Parmesan cheese: Parmigiano Reggiano is the Italian benchmark from the government designated controlled region of Northern Italy; made from cow's milk.

Pecorino cheese: A sharp Italian cheese made from sheep's milk. Used primarily for grating. The best is imported from Italy.

Porcini mushrooms (*Boletus edulis*): Found wild in forests, these are usually found dried in your marketplace. Called for in recipes because of their intense flavor. Soak in warm water about 30 minutes and use this liquid in the recipe along with the mushrooms.

Romano cheese: A hard grating cheese made from sheep's milk. It is sharper in flavor than Parmesan. Although the best is imported from Italy, Romano is also manufactured domestically.

Salt: Regular table salt is used, but by all means try the variety of sea salts.

Scallions/green onions: Cut from the white tip up to three-quarters into the green; discard the rest.

Spices and herbs: If a recipe calls for fresh herbs and you want to use dried, divide fresh herb measurement by 3. Example: 1 tablespoon fresh equals 1 teaspoon dried (1 tablespoon = 3 teaspoons). And vice versa. When recipe calls for dried and you want to use fresh herbs, multiply dried herb measurement by 3.

Note: Dried cilantro, parsley, and mint are not recommended for use since they do not have the flavor of their fresh counterparts.

Spices and herbs should be stored in a cool, dry area away from heat and direct sun. Purchase spices in small quantities to ensure their flavor will be alive and vibrant when added to recipes. You might start a spice-sharing club with friends so all can enjoy a steady and assorted collection of aromatics. It's fun to experiment and taste the creative employment of herbs and spices. For instance, coriander sprinkled on fresh corn on the cob highlights its sweetness and you will be able to forget the saltshaker.

I like to keep a couple of pots of my favorite herbs on the windowsill, not only to add green to the environment but so that they are readily available to use for cooking and garnishing. Mom and Dad grew basil and kept me, and many of my friends, supplied with this fragrant herb. I never seem to have enough of it, partly because of my ravenous appetite for pesto, that heavenly basil sauce that I dab on broiled fish, steaks, chops, and chicken.

There was a time when I made sauce in the service; Mom and Dad's basil joined the Army! I was home on leave, due back to prepare the weekend meals at a small company mess hall. Armed with extra virgin olive oil and fresh basil, I created a sauce. That Sunday I watched the guys as they devoured my sauce in my "four-star mess hall."

Every time a dried herb such as thyme, parsley, or basil is added to a recipe, it should be ground between your fingers to release the natural oil and bouquet. Never ever shake a dried herb directly into a pot cooking on the stove; steam will enter the jar and cause the contents to deteriorate.

Squid: If you buy fresh squid, you can cut it any way you'd like and enjoy the whole fillet instead of buying it frozen and cut up. Most important: *do not overcook.*

Toasted nuts: Just add nuts (whatever the recipe calls for) to a hot skillet and move them around with a spatula until they turn a toasty brown. Large nuts like walnut halves can be toasted in the oven at 350°F for about 8 to 10 minutes.

Tomatoes, canned plum: Marzano, Italy, is known for its plum tomatoes, which are commercially packed in a variety of ways and exported. Of course, California is also a major packer. Usually plum tomatoes are canned with juice. Some are canned in a heavier puree. Experiment with brands of your choosing.

Tomatoes, canned whole and peeled: Uncooked whole tomatoes are packed in tomato puree or tomato juice.

Tomato paste: Made from tomatoes that were cooked for several hours, strained, and reduced to a thick concentrate.

Tomato puree: Tomatoes are cooked briefly and strained to make a puree with a fairly thick consistency.

Tomato sauce: Cooked tomatoes with the addition of seasoning and sometimes tomato paste.

Wine: As I've said so many times, *There's no such thing as a cooking wine. Use the same wine you are going to drink to cook with.* One of my favorite Italian brands is from the Bolla family.

FREEZING

Keep a roll of masking tape, a marker, and, my preference, waxed freezer paper placed conveniently near the freezer for wrapping and labeling fresh meat items. We all know how difficult it is to remove aluminum foil from frozen meats, so for optimum storage, rewrap supermarket meats in waxed freezer wrap. Many people opt to use plastic freezer bags.

Wrap meat in small portions of one or two servings. It is very easy to defrost more than one portion if needed, but very hard to break one frozen burger or chop from a mass of frozen meat. When buying chopped meat for the freezer, portion and form it into patties before freezing.

Strong plastic freezer bags are good for vegetables. Take advantage of low seasonal prices on various vegetables and blanch and freeze them when they are in their prime. At mealtime, remove what is needed and mix with other vegetables for a garden assortment.

Keep order in your freezer! And keep it clean, thus avoiding any odors that are hard to get rid of. Keep an open plastic container filled with baking soda in the freezer to eliminate odors. Label everything wrapped with quantity and date, and be sure to use older items first. One of the most distressing things that can happen with your frozen food is freezer burn. It can be prevented if items are wrapped properly and rotated.

If your freezer can accommodate large quantities of food, it may be a good idea to use my inventory system. On large index cards, list each package with its contents, quantity, and date frozen. Mark each package with a number that is listed on your index cards. This way, instead of doing the "freezer shuffle" when you need to browse, just look over your card or cards and plan from your easy chair; it saves time, labor, and money! Don't forget to cross off what you take out and to add new items.

SUGGESTED CARD FILE SYSTEM

No.	Category	Item	Date
#06	Cooked meals (Leftovers)	1 Chicken Caprese	Aug. 18
#07	Vegetables	Approx. 2 cups squash	Sept. 10
#08	Meat	1 large turkey leg with thigh meat	July 19

Now you will always be prepared to have a satisfying meal even when the clock is against you or you are not in the mood for cooking with love.

The following list gives suggested lengths of time for storing frozen foods, provided they were properly frozen and correctly wrapped and the freezer environment is at a constant 0°F. A thermometer for the freezer is a good investment.

MAXIMUM STORAGE TIME AT 0°F
FOR FROZEN FOODS

Vegetables, plain	12 months
Vegetables, sauced	6 months
Fruits	12 months
Precooked frozen dinners	6–8 months
Most fish	6 months
Poultry	8 months
Meat, ground or organ	3–4 months
Meat, whole cuts	6–8 months

When planning your errands, do your grocery shopping last, and when in the supermarket, pick up your frozen items last. Inspect for signs of telltale defrosting, such as peas clumped together in plastic bags, boxes that are out of shape, ice cream oozing out of containers.

Avoid buying frozen groceries that are sitting on the supermarket floor waiting to be placed in the freezer.

Keep all frozen items packed together, preferably in an insulated bag, if available. I always keep a large cooler in the trunk of my car for transporting the frozen foods during the trip home. The cooler also comes in handy when I bring food to friends, tasters, and local television appearances; and for taking home some of goodies. Put the frozen foods away as soon as you get home, and remember to add them to your index system.

In winter, put groceries in the trunk, where it is cold; in summer, put them up front with you. If you leave your groceries behind at the store for delivery, take the frozen items with you.

Always, always keep in mind the outdoor temperature when you are driving your frozen and fresh foods home from the store. We all have had butter and ice cream melt in summer heat, but I once had the opposite experience in Lacrosse, Wisconsin, where I was due to make a live appearance on the *Noon News*. I drove from Minneapolis the night before the show, in good -10°F winter weather. Without thinking, I left all the groceries in the trunk of the car.

The next morning, I gathered my props and, after an hour in the heated studio, I reached for an egg. I banged it gently against the bowl to break the shell—nothing happened. I banged a little harder and still nothing, so I banged much harder. The bowl broke and peach cream poured over the table. The egg was frozen solid. I continued to walk through the recipe; luckily, I had the finished dish ready to show on camera.

Never defrost food that needs refrigeration outside of the refrigerator. Plan ahead to allow enough time for defrosting in the refrigerator or follow your microwave directions for defrosting. Most raw frozen foods, once defrosted, can be cooked and then refrozen later.

PLAN-AHEAD FREEZER MEALS

It's a good idea to keep cooked chicken parts in your freezer. I like chicken or turkey breast cutlets, three-quarters cooked, individually wrapped, that I can pop under the broiler or microwave with a topping of Parmesan cheese, zucchini, tarragon, lemon, oil, onions, or whatever. Wrap tightly and freeze. When you are looking for a snack or munchie, there it is.

With proper freezer use, you can cook one day and eat for four days.

Passing down recipes from generation to generation results in what I call good cooking; the rest of the world calls it gourmet cooking. The more we experiment and taste different foods, the more we want to discover new tastes and combinations.

CHAPTER ONE

Appetizers

ANTIPASTO

Italian Chicken Salad

Prosciutto Wrapped Arugula

Spinach Stuffed Clams

Stuffed Mussels

Mussels and Sausages

Eggs in Tuna Sauce

Broiled Shrimp with Red Pepper Sauce

Parchment Asparagus with Prosciutto

Roman Artichokes

Eggplant Dip

Beef Carpaccio

Stuffed Mushrooms with Fontina

Italian Chicken Salad

What's so special about chicken salad? you're thinking. Well, this Italian Chicken Salad will knock your socks off! It starts with a roasted chicken (to save time, you can even cheat and buy it already cooked). Poached chicken breasts can't compare to the taste of roasted whole chicken with the flavor combination of white and dark meat!

1   2-pound roasted chicken
1   fennel bulb, cored and thinly sliced
1   small red onion, thinly sliced
3   celery stalks, thinly sliced on a bias
½   cup extra virgin olive oil
3   cloves garlic, chopped
    Juice of 2 lemons
½   cup chopped fresh Italian parsley
½   cup mayonnaise
    Zest of 1 lemon
    Salt to taste
    Freshly ground black pepper to taste
1   bunch arugula, about 8 ounces, washed and dried

SERVES 6

Remove the meat from the chicken and shred it into bite-sized pieces. In a large bowl, combine the chicken, fennel, red onion, and celery and toss. Set aside.

In a skillet, heat the olive oil over moderate heat, add the garlic and sauté until golden. As soon as the garlic has colored, add the lemon juice all at once. Remove from heat and set aside to cool; then add to the chicken mixture. Add the parsley, mayonnaise, zest, salt, and pepper. Serve on a bed of arugula.

PER SERVING

| Calories 502 | Protein 22.1 grams | Carbohydrate 8.8 grams |
| Fiber 2.7 grams | Fat 42.9 grams | Net Carbs 6.1 grams |

Prosciutto Wrapped Arugula

You'll enjoy this make-ahead party item that is perfect for cocktails. For this recipe, buy only the best prosciutto you can find. The prosciutto from Parma, Italy, is the one by which all Italian ham is measured; some Italian companies have opened plants in the United States and are producing excellent domestic hams. The key here is to buy the best you can afford, since the ham is what you taste in this recipe.

1   pound arugula leaves or small spinach leaves,
     washed and dried thoroughly
1   tablespoon minced shallots
1   tablespoon Lemon Vinaigrette *(page 75)*
4   thin slices prosciutto, cut into 1-inch strips

YIELDS APPROXIMATELY 24 BUNDLES

In a mixing bowl, toss the arugula and shallots with the Lemon Vinaigrette. Make small bundles with the arugula by gathering a few leaves at the stems. Secure by wrapping a strip of prosciutto around the stems.

PER SERVING

Calories 11	Protein .81 grams	Carbohydrate .77 grams
Fiber .31 grams	Fat .69 grams	Net Carbs .46 grams

Spinach Stuffed Clams

This delicious starter can also be made with oysters. Your main course likely would be fish, but this is also a great appetizer with a beef course.

¼   **cup olive oil, divided**
32   **large cherrystone or Manila clams (about 2 pounds), scrubbed**
½   **cup white wine**
    Sautéed Spinach *(page 96)*, **reduce by half**
1   **cup White Sauce** *(page 79)*
¼   **cup grated Parmesan cheese**
2   **tablespoons chopped fresh Italian parsley**
    Salt to taste
    Freshly ground black pepper to taste

YIELDS 32

In a large skillet with a tight-fitting lid, heat half of the olive oil over moderately high heat. Add the clams; sauté until they start to open. Add the wine, cover, and steam until all the clams open, about 5 to 8 minutes. Discard any unopened clams. Transfer the clams to a shallow bowl until cool enough to handle. Remove the clam from its shell; put it on one of the half shells and discard the other. Arrange the clams on a baking sheet and chill.

Preheat the broiler. Squeeze any excess moisture from the spinach. Chop the spinach and put in a large bowl. Add White Sauce, Parmesan, and parsley and mix until well combined. Season to taste with salt and pepper. Mound the spinach stuffing on top of the clams. Broil the clams until hot and bubbly, 3 to 5 minutes. Cool slightly and serve.

PER SERVING

Calories 45   Protein 2.3 grams   Carbohydrate 1.3 grams
Fiber .31 grams   Fat 3.3 grams   New Carbs 1 gram

Stuffed Mussels

*This is an easy top-of-stove recipe. I try to cook this dish with
the same wine I will be serving with dinner.*

6	tablespoons extra virgin olive oil, divided
4	thin slices pancetta, minced
½	cup thinly sliced yellow onion
4	fresh plum tomatoes, finely chopped
3	tablespoons fresh Italian parsley, divided
	Salt to taste
	Freshly ground black pepper
18	mussels, scrubbed and debearded
1	clove garlic, minced
1	bay leaf
½	cup white wine

YIELDS 18

In a skillet, heat 2 tablespoons of olive oil and sauté the pancetta and yellow onion until the onion is translucent. Add the tomatoes, 1 tablespoon of parsley, salt, and pepper, and continue to cook for 5 minutes. Set aside in a bowl.

Wash and dry the skillet. Heat 2 tablespoons of olive oil in the skillet and add the mussels, 1 tablespoon parsley, garlic, bay leaf, salt, and pepper. As the mussels start to open, add white wine, cover, and steam for 5 minutes or until all the mussels have opened. (Discard any mussels that do not open.) Cool the mussels and any cooking liquid in a bowl. When the mussels are cool enough to handle, remove the mussel meat and reserve one half of the shell from each.

Put one mussel on each shell, and divide the tomato mixture among the mussels. Sprinkle the mussels with the remaining parsley, and drizzle 1 tablespoon of the cooking liquid over them. Chill until ready to serve. Drizzle each with the remaining oil and serve immediately.

PER SERVING

Calories 67	Protein 2.2 grams	Carbohydrate 1.6 grams
Fiber .23 grams	Fat 5.4 grams	Net Carbs 1.4 grams

Mussels and Sausages

This appetizer is equally great as a starter for either fish or meat. The secret is not to overcook the mussels. One rainy afternoon off the beaten path in Rome, I walked into a small family restaurant and was served this dish with fantastic bread (no bread now), some house wine, and a lot of smiles.

3	tablespoons extra virgin olive oil
½	cup chopped yellow onion
½	cup chopped green bell pepper
4	cloves garlic, chopped
4	sweet Italian sausages, cut into ½-inch slices
¼	pound prosciutto
4	fresh plum tomatoes, seeded and chopped
½	cup white wine
¼	teaspoon red pepper flakes
	Salt to taste
	Freshly ground black pepper to taste
2	pounds mussels, scrubbed and debearded
¼	cup chopped fresh Italian parsley

SERVES 6

In a large deep skillet, heat the oil over moderate heat. Add the yellow onion, bell pepper, and garlic and sauté for 5 minutes or until onion is translucent. Add the sausages and prosciutto, and cook until sausages are no longer pink. Add tomatoes, wine, pepper flakes, salt, and pepper. Reduce heat to low and simmer 20 minutes.

Arrange mussels on top of the sausage mixture, cover, and simmer for 5 minutes or until the mussels open. (Discard any mussels with unopened shells.) Transfer mussels to a large shallow serving dish, pour sausages and sauce over them, and sprinkle with parsley.

PER SERVING

Calories 443	Protein 35 grams	Carbohydrate 11.3 grams
Fiber 1 gram	Fat 27 grams	Net Carbs 10.3 grams

Eggs in Tuna Sauce

Slightly more expensive, but by all means worth the cost, Italian tuna fish packed in olive oil has a taste unmatched by any other canned tuna. Also remember that tuna packed in oil has a better taste than tuna packed in water.

6	ounces mayonnaise
4	ounces tuna packed in olive oil
3	tablespoons capers
2	anchovies
2	tablespoons freshly squeezed lemon juice
2	tablespoons heavy cream
½	teaspoon Dijon mustard
	Freshly ground black pepper to taste
4	hardboiled eggs, sliced ¼-inch thick
2	tablespoons chopped fresh parsley

SERVES 4

In a blender or food processor, combine the mayonnaise, tuna, 2 tablespoons capers, anchovies, lemon juice, cream, mustard, and pepper. Purée until smooth and set aside.

Arrange the sliced eggs on a serving platter and drizzle the tuna sauce over the top. Garnish with the remaining tablespoon of capers and the parsley.

PER SERVING

Calories 470	Protein 15.3 grams	Carbohydrate 3 grams
Fiber .31 grams	Fat 44.4 grams	Net Carbs 2.7 grams

Broiled Shrimp with Red Pepper Sauce

*Recently I made several TV appearances in Florida and the West Coast
on which this recipe was shown. Great party food! Rather than clean
pounds of shrimp, I found some fabulous flash-frozen, cleaned shrimp,
which made this dish even easier. You can also have your fishmonger
clean them for you—that's if you have a fish store near you.*

2	tablespoons freshly squeezed lemon juice
1	tablespoon chopped fresh Italian parsley
1	teaspoon chopped garlic
¼	teaspoon red pepper flakes
	Salt to taste
	Freshly ground black pepper to taste
½	cup extra virgin olive oil
1	pound large shrimp, peeled and deveined
	Roasted Red Bell Pepper Sauce *(page 81)*

YIELDS 18 PIECES

In a medium bowl, whisk together the lemon juice, parsley, garlic,
pepper flakes, salt, and pepper. Whisking constantly, gradually add
the olive oil in a thin stream. Add the shrimp and toss to coat. Cover
and marinate for at least 30 minutes in the refrigerator.

Preheat the broiler. Drain the marinade from the shrimp and
arrange them on a rack set over a baking sheet. Broil until the shrimp
are pink and firm to the touch, 3 to 5 minutes. Serve with Red Bell
Pepper Sauce on the side for dipping.

PER SERVING

Calories 116	Protein 5.9 grams	Carbohydrate 2.4 grams
Fiber .65 grams	Fat 9.4 grams	Net Carbs 1.8 grams

Parchment Asparagus with Prosciutto

Cooking in parchment offers an alternative to pastry, which adds carbs. In this recipe the star is the asparagus, with the silky prosciutto steamed and cooked to perfection.

24   thin spears of asparagus, trimmed and cut
     to about 6 inches in length
3   tablespoons butter plus 1 teaspoon for the parchment
4   thin slices prosciutto
½   cup grated Parmesan cheese
     Salt to taste
     Freshly ground black pepper to taste
½   cup white wine

YIELDS 24

Preheat the oven to 350°F. Bring a large pot of salted water to a boil and prepare a large bowl of ice water. Add the asparagus and boil until just tender, but still crisp. Transfer immediately to the ice water to stop the cooking process. Drain, pat dry, and set aside.

Cut 4 pieces of parchment into 10-inch by 10-inch squares and butter lightly. Lay a piece of parchment on the work surface and put a slice of prosciutto in the center. Sprinkle with cheese; then arrange 6 asparagus spears on top. Sprinkle with more cheese; then season with salt and pepper. Wrap the prosciutto around the asparagus bundles; then wrap the entire bundle with the parchment. Repeat this procedure for the remaining rolls.

In a large ovenproof skillet with a tight-fitting lid, melt the butter over moderate heat, and arrange the bundles, seam-side down, in the pan. Pour the wine over the bundles, cover, and cook the asparagus in the oven for 15 minutes or until the parchment starts to color. Remove from pan, and unwrap carefully to avoid being burned by the escaping hot steam. Arrange in the center of a plate, and sprinkle with the remaining cheese.

PER SERVING

Calories 27	Protein 1.3 grams	Carbohydrate .61 grams
Fiber .24 grams	Fat 2.3 grams	Net Carbs .37 grams

Roman Artichokes

This is a unique appetizer I experienced last year in the Old Roman Jewish Quarter in Italy. I was so impressed by this interesting dish that I set about re-creating it when I got home. The following recipe comes very close to matching my Italian experience.

4 medium-sized globe artichokes
1 lemon, cut in half
 Olive oil for frying
 Salt to taste
 Freshly ground black pepper to taste

SERVES 4

Remove the coarse outer leaves from the artichokes, periodically rubbing the artichoke with the lemon, until the yellowish green leaves are revealed. Using a vegetable peeler, remove the skin from the stem and outer leaves, continuing to rub with lemon. Trim ¼ inch from the end of the stem; then spread the leaves of the artichoke open. Expose the choke and press the center to hold the leaves open. Using a small teaspoon, remove the prickly and fuzzy interior of the artichoke.

In a straight-sided saucepan large enough to hold all the artichokes without crowding, heat enough oil to come 2½ to 3 inches up the side of the pan to 350°F. Carefully put the artichokes into the oil, leaves out and choke down. Fry until golden on all sides. Transfer to paper towels to drain and cool. Season with the salt and pepper and serve.

PER SERVING

Calories 179	Protein 4.2 grams	Carbohydrate 13.4 grams
Fiber 6.5 grams	Fat 13.7 grams	Net Carbs 6.9 grams

Eggplant Dip

*Eggplant makes a tasty, low-carb dip that everyone will love.
Serve this dip and I guarantee it will vanish like magic. Just be sure to toast the
pine nuts; it makes a difference in the final taste. It's easy—just add the nuts to a hot
skillet and move them around with a spatula until they turn a toasty brown.*

1   medium eggplant
2   garlic cloves, chopped
1   tablespoon fresh lemon juice
1   tablespoon chopped fresh basil plus one whole leaf
      (for garnish), or 1 teaspoon dried basil
1   tablespoon pine nuts, toasted
¼   cup extra virgin olive oil
      Salt to taste

VEGETABLES
2   carrots, cut into wide ribbons
1   medium red bell pepper, cored, seeded,
      and cut into ¼-inch strips
2   stalks celery, halved and cut into sticks

YIELDS 30 SERVINGS

Preheat oven to 450°F.

Prick the eggplant in several places with the tines of a fork and put on a baking sheet. Roast eggplant for 20 minutes or until collapsed and no longer firm to the touch. Set aside until cool enough to handle; then remove peel and discard. Cool pulp completely.

In a food processor, combine eggplant, garlic, lemon juice, basil, and pine nuts and pulse until well combined and nuts are chopped. With the processor running, add the olive oil slowly in a thin stream. Add salt, garnish with basil leaf, and serve with vegetables for dipping.

PER SERVING

Calories 25	Protein .32 grams	Carbohydrate 1.7 grams
Fiber .60 grams	Fat 2 grams	Net Carbs 1.1 grams

Beef Carpaccio

This dish was invented for an exhibition of an Italian Renaissance painter. Carpaccio is the Italian answer to beef tartare. I don't know who came up with the idea of eating raw beef, but I'm glad they did. Be sure you use beef from a reliable butcher, prepare this dish quickly, and keep it refrigerated until you serve it. It must be chilled. Remember, the vegetables should be cut thin, thin.

8	ounces beef tenderloin
4	teaspoons capers
2	stalks celery, sliced thinly on the bias
½	small red onion, slivered
2	tablespoons fresh Italian parsley
½	cup extra virgin olive oil
	Juice and zest of 2 lemons
	Salt to taste
	Freshly ground black pepper
¼	cup mayonnaise

SERVES 4

Cut the beef tenderloin across the grain into four pieces. Put a piece of beef between two pieces of plastic wrap and pound gently with a meat mallet until very thin and nearly transparent. Leave the beef in the plastic wrap, and repeat with the remaining pieces. Chill beef in the plastic wrap until ready to serve.

Just before serving, peel one layer of plastic from the beef. Turn the beef over onto a chilled serving plate, uncovered side facing down. Peel the remaining plastic wrap away. Repeat this process with the remaining beef and plates. Divide and sprinkle the capers, celery, red onion, and parsley evenly between the four plates. Drizzle with olive oil and lemon juice and sprinkle with zest, dividing these evenly among the plates. Season with salt and pepper. Put a dollop of mayonnaise in the center of each plate and serve immediately.

PER SERVING

Calories 506	Protein 10.8 grams	Carbohydrate 4.2 grams
Fiber .87 grams	Fat 50.3 grams	Net Carbs 3.3 grams

Stuffed Mushrooms with Fontina

Stuffed mushrooms are always a crowd-pleaser; here, prosciutto and fontina cheese really add flavor. You'll love these. They can be a light meal in themselves if served with a nice salad. The cream bath keeps them from shrinking.

2   tablespoons plus 2 teaspoons olive oil
1   tablespoon dried porcini mushrooms (about ⅛ ounce)
¼   cup warm water
12 large white mushrooms, wiped clean
    Salt to taste
    Freshly ground black pepper
1–2 cups half-and-half
¼   cup chopped scallions
¼   cup chopped prosciutto
1   tablespoon chopped fresh Italian parsley
½   cup coarsely grated fontina cheese

YIELDS 12

Preheat oven to 375°F. Brush a shallow baking dish large enough to hold the mushrooms with olive oil.

Put the dried mushrooms in a small bowl and cover with ¼ cup warm water. Let mushrooms soak for 20 minutes; then squeeze excess water back into the bowl and reserve. Chop the soaked mushrooms and set aside.

Remove stems from the white mushrooms; coarsely chop and set aside. Brush all surfaces of the mushroom caps with olive oil. Put in prepared baking dish and sprinkle with salt and pepper. Pour in the cream, which should come to the top of the mushrooms just below the stuffing.

Heat 2 tablespoons olive oil in a medium skillet. Add soaked mushrooms, chopped mushroom stems, and scallions and sauté until stems are soft and the mixture is dry. Add reserved soaking liquid, prosciutto, parsley, salt, and pepper and continue to cook until all liquid has evaporated.

Divide mixture evenly among mushroom caps and sprinkle with fontina. Bake until cheese is golden, about 15 to 18 minutes.

PER SERVING

Calories 77	Protein 3.9 grams	Carbohydrate 2.8 grams
Fiber .53 grams	Fat 5.2 grams	Net Carbs 2.3 grams

CHAPTER TWO

Soups and Stews

ZUPPA UMIDI

Cream of Tomato Soup with Basil

Hearty Tomato and Kale Soup

Chicken Soup with Vegetables

Clam Soup

Roasted Eggplant Soup

Mushroom Soup with Tomatoes

Spinach Soup

Onion Soup with Almonds and Cinnamon

Zucchini Soup

Fish Soup

Minestrone Soup

Mushroom Soup

Chicken Stock

Fish Stock

Cauliflower Soup with Pesto

Lamb Stew

Beef Stew Abruzzi Style

Cream of Tomato Soup with Basil

The mix of fresh and canned tomatoes creates a heady tomato flavor, spiked with white wine and cream, perfumed with fresh basil (which should be growing in your garden or on your kitchen windowsill) just like in Naples.

2	medium yellow onions, finely chopped
2	cloves garlic, crushed
¼	cup extra virgin olive oil
1	teaspoon red pepper flakes
1	28-ounce can whole peeled tomatoes
	Salt to taste
	Freshly ground pepper to taste
1	teaspoon fresh Italian parsley, chopped
¼	cup dry white wine
6	fresh tomatoes, coarsely chopped
1	quart Chicken Stock (*page 61*)
6	fresh basil leaves
¼	cup heavy cream

YIELDS APPROXIMATELY 2 QUARTS; SERVES 10

In a large pot, sauté the yellow onions and garlic in the olive oil. Add the red pepper flakes and canned tomatoes, season with salt and pepper, and add the Italian parsley. Allow to cook for 10 to 15 minutes and deglaze with the white wine; reduce by half. Then add the fresh tomatoes and stock. Simmer for 30 minutes and puree in a blender with the basil leaves. If the soup seems thin, return to the stove to reduce, and add the cream just before serving.

PER SERVING

Calories 109	Protein 1.7 grams	Carbohydrate 8 grams
Fiber 1.7 grams	Fat 8 grams	Net Carbs 6.4 grams

Hearty Tomato and Kale Soup

If you've never eaten kale, you're in for a treat. This heavy green leafy vegetable is high in iron and vitamins and imparts a flavor much like cabbage. This hearty soup is perfect on its own for lunch, or as a first course at dinner.

½	cup olive oil
1	medium yellow onion, sliced
1	medium leek, sliced
3	cloves garlic, chopped
1	bunch kale, washed and dried
8	fresh plum tomatoes, peeled, seeded, and chopped
1	teaspoon red pepper flakes
	Salt to taste
	Freshly ground black pepper to taste
1	cup canned crushed tomatoes
3	cups water
1	tablespoon chopped fresh Italian parsley
1	teaspoon chopped fresh thyme or a pinch of dried thyme
	Grated Parmesan cheese for sprinkling

SERVES 6

In a large soup pot, heat the olive oil over moderate heat and sauté the onion and leek until they are soft, about 5 minutes. Add the garlic and sauté for 2 minutes. Remove the stems from the kale and chop the leaves. Add the kale to the pot along with the fresh tomatoes, red pepper flakes, salt, and pepper. Cook on medium heat for 10 minutes. Add the canned tomatoes, water, parsley, and thyme. Bring the soup to a boil, then reduce the heat and simmer 45 minutes. Adjust the seasoning and serve with Parmesan cheese on the side.

PER SERVING

Calories 220	Protein 2.8 grams	Carbohydrate 13.3 grams
Fiber 2.7 grams	Fat 18.7 grams	Net Carbs 10.6 grams

Chicken Soup with Vegetables

Chicken soup really is good for the soul—especially the way my Aunt Mary makes it. She says the recipe comes from her cousin in Naples. The great taste comes from roasting the chicken first.

½ cup extra virgin olive oil
2 cups cooked chicken *(see Lemon Roast Chicken, page 177)*
1 cup yellow onion, sliced
2 stalks celery, diced
1 medium carrot, diced
1 medium leek, split and diced
2 cloves garlic
1 teaspoon red pepper flakes
½ medium bunch Swiss chard, stemmed and chopped
4 ounces green beans, cut in 1-inch lengths
1 quart Chicken Stock *(page 61)*
1 sprig fresh rosemary or a pinch of dried rosemary
½ cup peas, fresh or frozen
  Salt to taste
  Freshly ground black pepper to taste

YIELDS APPROXIMATELY 2 QUARTS;
SERVES 10 AS AN APPETIZER

Heat the oil in a large pot; add the yellow onion, celery, carrot, and leek. Cook until the vegetables start to soften. Add the garlic and red pepper flakes; then add the chard, green beans, stock, peas, and rosemary. Adjust the seasoning and allow to simmer for half an hour.

PER SERVING

Calories 180	Protein 9.6 grams	Carbohydrate 6.4 grams
Fiber 1.7 grams	Fat 13.2 grams	Net Carbs 4.7 grams

Clam Soup

I first tasted this soup in the port town of Sorrento, Italy, while looking for inspiration for new recipes for this book. I've eaten clam soup my whole life, but I think it's the combination of fennel and tomato that makes this fragrant soup so special. It's a light soup that makes a satisfying light meal or first course. Canned clams work well, but fresh Manila clams make this soup a five-star dish.

½   cup olive oil, divided
2   cloves garlic, minced
1   teaspoon red pepper flakes
3   pounds fresh Manila clams, washed
1   cup white wine
½   cup chopped fresh Italian parsley, divided
1   small yellow onion, diced
1   stalk celery, diced
1   small bulb fennel, trimmed and diced
1   small leek, split and diced
     Salt to taste
     Freshly ground black pepper to taste
4   fresh tomatoes, peeled and diced
1   quart Fish Stock *(page 62)*

YIELDS APPROXIMATELY 2 QUARTS;
SERVES 10 AS AN APPETIZER

In a large sauté pan, heat ¼ cup of the olive oil and sauté half of the garlic with the red pepper flakes. Add the clams and sauté until the clams start to open; add the wine and half of the parsley. Cover, reduce heat to low, and simmer for 10 minutes. Once the clams have steamed open, remove them from the shells and set aside. Strain the cooking liquid and reserve for the soup.

In a large pot, heat the remaining olive oil and sauté the onion, celery, fennel, and leek. Season and allow to cook until the vegetables become soft. Add the remaining garlic, the clams and cooking liquid, tomatoes, fish stock, and remaining parsley. Allow to simmer for 30 minutes.

PER SERVING

Calories 321	Protein 32.6 grams	Carbohydrate 11.1 grams
Fiber 1.4 grams	Fat 14.1 grams	Net Carbs 9.7 grams

Roasted Eggplant Soup

I know you are probably thinking, What, eggplant soup? Just try it, you'll love it even though eggplant is not a traditional soup ingredient. I discovered this recipe in the Ortegia in the Old City of Siracusa in a tiny, off-the-beaten-track restaurant. The food was so inventive, and this soup was the highlight of the meal. This dish can be made vegetarian by substituting vegetable stock.

3	large eggplants
2	cloves garlic, crushed
1	small red onion, sliced
¼	cup extra virgin olive oil
2	stalks celery
1	28-ounce can whole peeled tomatoes
5	fresh basil leaves, plus extra for garnish, or 1 teaspoon dried basil
¼	cup chopped fresh Italian parsley
	Salt to taste
	Freshly ground black pepper
1	quart Chicken Stock *(page 61)*
½	cup grated Parmesan cheese

YIELDS APPROXIMATELY 2 QUARTS;
SERVES 10 AS AN APPETIZER

Pierce the eggplants with a dinner fork and bake on a sheet pan in a 350°F oven for 30 minutes. Once the eggplants are soft, slice in half and remove the flesh with a large metal spoon. Set aside and allow to cool. In a large pot, sauté the garlic and red onion in the olive oil. Once the onion is opaque, add the celery, tomatoes, basil, and parsley. Season to taste and add the eggplants and stock. Allow to simmer for about 45 minutes. Purée the soup in a blender, add the Parmesan cheese, and adjust seasoning. Serve with fresh basil.

PER SERVING

Calories 152	Protein 5.3 grams	Carbohydrate 19.5 grams
Fiber 7 grams	Fat 7.4 grams	Net Carbs 12.5

Mushroom Soup with Tomatoes

Tomatoes make a tasty soup base because they bring out the best in other vegetables, as well as complementary meats and fish, but they work especially well with mushrooms. In fact, this is one of my favorite soups because it contains my all-time favorite vegetables—tomatoes and mushrooms. Mangia!

½   cup extra virgin olive oil, more if needed
½   pound shiitake mushrooms, stems removed and sliced
½   pound button mushrooms, sliced
1   small yellow onion, chopped
2   cloves garlic, crushed
    Salt to taste
    Freshly ground black pepper to taste
1   bunch fresh thyme, or 2 teaspoons dried thyme
1   teaspoon fresh oregano or a pinch of dried oregano
½   cup white wine
6   fresh plum tomatoes, peeled and diced
1   quart Chicken Stock (*page 61*)
1   tablespoon white vinegar
1   tablespoon tomato paste
¼   cup chopped fresh Italian parsley

YIELDS APPROXIMATELY 2 QUARTS;
SERVES 10 AS AN APPETIZER

In a large pot, heat the oil and sauté the mushrooms (add more oil if necessary). Once the mushrooms are cooked, set aside, and in the same pan sauté the onion and garlic in some additional oil, season, add the herbs and the mushrooms. Increase the heat and deglaze with the white wine. Add the fresh tomatoes, stock, vinegar, and tomato paste. Allow to simmer for 30 to 45 minutes. Add the parsley and serve.

PER SERVING

Calories 43	Protein 1.9 grams	Carbohydrate 6.4 grams
Fiber 1.2 grams	Fat .5 grams	Net Carbs 5.2 grams

Spinach Soup

*Traditionally this is served in Italy with Arborio rice, but this
low-carb version tastes good even without it.*

1½ pounds fresh spinach
    (or 2 10-ounce packages frozen),
    washed and chopped
6 cups Chicken Stock *(page 61)*
1 clove garlic, crushed
½ teaspoon ground nutmeg
1 tablespoon fresh lemon juice
    Freshly ground black pepper to taste
    Salt to taste *(optional)*
¼ cup grated Romano cheese

SERVES 6

If fresh spinach is used, it must be cleaned thoroughly and chopped.
Place the stock, garlic, and spinach in a large saucepan. Bring to boil,
then add the nutmeg, lemon juice, pepper, and salt and simmer until
the spinach is cooked. Serve with a sprinkling of Romano cheese.

PER SERVING

Calories 75	Protein 8.9 grams	Carbohydrate 5.4 grams
Fiber 3.1 grams	Fat 2.4 grams	Net Carbs 2.3 grams

Onion Soup with Almonds and Cinnamon

When you visit sunny Sicily, you are in for a variety of original dishes that span the myriad cultures that occupied this island. This soup is one that is influenced by its Arab conquerors.

½	cup olive oil
6	medium yellow onions, sliced
	Salt to taste
	Freshly ground black pepper
1	clove garlic, chopped
1	cup sliced almonds, plus 2 tablespoons for garnish
2	quarts Chicken Stock *(page 61)*
1	teaspoon ground cinnamon

SERVES 10 AS AN APPETIZER

In a large heavy saucepan, heat the oil over moderate heat. Sauté the onions with a pinch of salt and pepper, 5 to 8 minutes or until translucent. Increase the heat and cook until the onions are golden and begin to caramelize, 10 to 15 minutes. Add the garlic and continue to cook until golden. Stir in the almonds; then add the stock, cinnamon, salt, and pepper. Bring the liquid to a boil; then reduce the heat to low and simmer for 45 to 60 minutes or until the onions are soft. Purée the soup in a blender in batches and adjust the seasoning with salt, pepper, and cinnamon.

PER SERVING

Calories 194	Protein 3.5 grams	Carbohydrate 8.8 grams
Fiber 2.5 grams	Fat 16.8 grams	Net Carbs 6.3 grams

Zucchini Soup

*From the same restaurant that invented the Roasted Eggplant Soup on page 53.
The idea of zucchini as a soup was new to me, so I went back for a second meal. This
soup ranks almost as high as the Roasted Eggplant Soup and has the added benefit
of giving you another way to use up all those zucchinis from your (or your neighbor's)
garden. By substituting vegetable stock, you can make this a vegetarian dish.*

¼ cup extra virgin olive oil
4 medium zucchinis, chopped
1 clove garlic, thinly sliced
½ cup white wine
3 cups Chicken Stock *(page 61)*
    Salt to taste
    Freshly ground black pepper to taste
½ cup half-and-half
½ teaspoon red pepper flakes
4 fresh basil leaves, chopped,
        or ½ teaspoon dried basil
½ cup Parmesan cheese

SERVES 4

In a medium saucepan, heat the olive oil over moderate heat and sauté
the zucchinis until they begin to soften, about 5 minutes. Add the garlic and cook until golden. Add the wine and let it bubble a minute;
then add the stock, salt, and pepper. Bring the soup to a boil; then
reduce the heat to low and simmer until the zucchinis are very soft,
about 10 to 15 minutes.

In a blender, purée the soup in batches until smooth. Return the
soup to the pan and gradually stir in the half-and-half and red pepper
flakes, and heat through gently. Stir in the basil and Parmesan cheese
and adjust the seasoning with salt and pepper. Serve immediately.

PER SERVING

| Calories 242 | Protein 8 grams | Carbohydrate 8.2 grams |
| Fiber 2.5 grams | Fat 20.3 grams | Net Carbs 5.7 grams |

Fish Soup

The Italian coastal towns all have an abundance of fresh fish, and each town has its particular fish soup recipes depending on which fish are the most plentiful in its area. I've taken my favorite and adapted it here. Remember, the fish you use has to be the freshest available; you will taste the difference.

¼	cup olive oil
1	medium yellow onion, sliced
1	clove garlic, sliced
1	teaspoon red pepper flakes
	Salt to taste
	Freshly ground black pepper to taste
½	cup white wine
8	mussels, scrubbed and debearded, or 8 clams, scrubbed
2	cups clam juice
2	tablespoons chopped fresh Italian parsley
8	ounces halibut, cut into bite-sized pieces
4	medium shrimp, peeled and deveined
4	leaves chopped fresh basil or ½ teaspoon dried basil
1	large fresh, ripe tomato, cored, seeded, and chopped

SERVES 4

In a large saucepan, heat the olive oil over moderately high heat and sauté the onion until the onion begins to turn gold, about 8 minutes. Add the garlic, pepper flakes, salt, and pepper and sauté another minute. Add the white wine and let it bubble a minute; then add the mussels or clams and cook until the shells begin to open. Add the clam juice and parsley, bring the liquid to a simmer, and add the halibut. Simmer until the flesh is opaque throughout; then add the shrimp. Discard any unopened mussels or clams. Simmer 10 minutes and serve garnished with basil and tomato.

PER SERVING

Calories 261	Protein 18 grams	Carbohydrate 6.7 grams
Fiber 1.2 grams	Fat 16 grams	Net Carbs 5.5 grams

Minestrone Soup

*Every Italian restaurant has a version of minestrone soup on the menu.
The original came from Ristorante Lo Scudiero in Palermo. My version
has no legumes, in order to keep the carb count low.*

½	cup olive oil
2	stalks celery, chopped
1	small carrot, chopped
1	small red onion, chopped
2	cloves garlic, chopped
3	small zucchinis, chopped
3	medium tomatoes, chopped
4	ounces fresh spinach, washed and coarsely chopped
6	large leaves Swiss chard, washed and cut into thin strips
4	ounces green beans, trimmed and cut into ½-inch lengths
¼	cup chopped fresh Italian parsley
	Salt to taste
	Freshly ground black pepper to taste
2	quarts Chicken Stock *(page 61)*
½	cup grated Parmesan cheese.

SERVES 10 AS AN APPETIZER

Heat the olive oil in a large soup pot over moderately high heat. Sauté
the celery, carrot, and onion, until the onion is translucent and softened. Add the garlic and sauté briefly. Add the zucchinis and tomatoes; cook, stirring occasionally, for 10 minutes. Add the spinach,
Swiss chard, green beans, parsley, salt, and pepper, and cook another
10 minutes. Add the chicken stock, bring to a boil, then reduce the
heat and simmer 30 minutes.

Adjust seasoning with salt and pepper and serve with Parmesan
cheese for sprinkling.

PER SERVING

Calories 176	Protein 7.6 grams	Carbohydrate 7.5 grams
Fiber 2.3 grams	Fat 13.5 grams	Net Carbs 5.2 grams

Mushroom Soup

Ah, creamy mushroom soup, flavorful and satisfying, with an Italian twist.
Next to chicken soup, this is my choice for a soothing light meal.

4   tablespoons butter
1   medium yellow onion, sliced
1   clove garlic, chopped
1   pound button mushrooms, wiped clean and sliced
1½ teaspoons chopped fresh thyme
      or ½ teaspoon dried thyme
    Salt to taste
    Freshly ground black pepper to taste
½   cup white wine
3   cups Chicken Stock *(page 61)* or
      3 cups canned chicken stock
1½ cups White Sauce *(page 00)*
½   cup grated Parmesan cheese
2   tablespoons chopped fresh Italian parsley

SERVES 6 AS AN APPETIZER

In a large soup pot, melt the butter over moderate heat and add the
onion and garlic. Sauté until the onion is translucent, about 5 minutes. Add the mushrooms, thyme, salt, pepper, wine, and stock and
cook over moderate heat until the mushrooms are tender, about 10
minutes. Stir in the White Sauce until well combined and cook
another 10 minutes. Carefully purée the soup in batches in a blender
or food processor. Reheat, adjust the seasoning with salt and pepper,
and blend in the Parmesan cheese. Garnish individual bowls with
parsley, and serve.

PER SERVING

Calories 270	Protein 10 grams	Carbohydrate 9 grams
Fiber 1.4 grams	Fat 19.6 grams	Net Carbs 7.6 grams

Chicken Stock

It is always a good idea to keep chicken stock frozen because you never know when you'll need it. The best way is to freeze it in various sizes of plastic freezer bags so you'll be ready when you need to prepare any recipe.

1   3–3½ pound chicken, rinsed
1½ gallons cold water
1   medium yellow onion, chopped
3   stalks celery, chopped
2   medium carrots, peeled and chopped
3   cloves garlic, cut in half
3   sprigs fresh Italian parsley
1   bay leaf

YIELDS APPROXIMATELY 1 GALLON

Put the water and chicken in a large stockpot. Add the remaining ingredients and slowly bring just to the boiling point. Lower the heat and cook uncovered at barely a simmer for 2 hours, skimming scum off the surface as needed.

Remove the chicken and cool. When cool enough to handle, remove the meat from the bones and set aside. The meat of the chicken can be used for other dishes such as Chicken Salad (page 35) or as an addition to soups.

Return the bones to the stockpot and simmer 1 more hour. Strain the broth through damp cheesecloth and set aside to cool. Discard the bones and vegetables. When the stock has cooled, refrigerate until ready to use in soups and sauces.

May be frozen for extended storage.

PER CUP

Calories 39	Protein 5 grams	Carbohydrate .93 gram
Fiber 0 grams	Fat 1.4 grams	Net Carbs .93 gram

Fish Stock

I find that when a recipe calls for fish stock, most people either skip the recipe or substitute water or wine, but by so doing, they compromise the finished dish. Here's an easy recipe you can make with discarded raw fish bones and trimmings, raw shrimp shells, et cetera. Just freeze in small quantities and you'll have it ready when your recipe calls for it. You'll add a new dimension to your cooking. Try it and see.

1½ gallons cold water
2½ pounds halibut bones
     or bones of another lean white fish, rinsed
2 stalks celery, chopped
1 medium yellow onion, chopped
1 medium leek, split and chopped
½ lemon
3 sprigs fresh Italian parsley
1 teaspoon black peppercorns
1 bay leaf

YIELDS APPROXIMATELY 1 GALLON

Put the water and the fish bones in a large stockpot over moderately high heat. Add the remaining ingredients and bring just to a boil. Immediately reduce the heat to barely a simmer and cook 20 minutes, skimming scum from the surface as necessary. Strain the stock through damp cheesecloth and set aside to cool. Chill in the refrigerator until ready to use. The stock will keep for up to four days. May be frozen for extended storage.

PER CUP

Calories 40	Protein 5.4 grams	Carbohydrate 0 grams
Fiber 0 grams	Fat 1.9 grams	Net Carbs 0 grams

Cauliflower Soup with Pesto

This recipe is a good example of why you should keep some pesto sauce frozen for future use. Two "ice cubes" of frozen pesto sauce is all you need for this recipe.

¼   cup extra virgin olive oil
2   tablespoons butter
1   medium yellow onion, chopped
2   cloves garlic, minced
1   medium head cauliflower, cored and diced
    Salt to taste
    Freshly ground black pepper to taste
¼   teaspoon nutmeg
1   tablespoon chopped fresh Italian parsley
1   quart Chicken Stock (*page 61*)
     or 1 quart canned chicken stock
1   cup White Sauce (*page 79*)
½   cup grated Parmesan cheese, plus some for sprinkling
¼   cup Pesto Sauce (*page 77*)

SERVES 6

In a medium saucepan, heat the olive oil and butter over moderate heat. Sauté the onion and garlic until the onion is translucent, about 5 minutes. Add the cauliflower, salt, pepper, nutmeg, and parsley, and stir well. Cook the cauliflower until softened; then add the Chicken Stock. Simmer for 20 minutes, or until the cauliflower is soft and the flavors have blended. Add the White Sauce and cook another 5 minutes. Purée the soup in batches in a blender or food processor until smooth. Add the Parmesan cheese to the last batch and purée. Combine the batches and stir well, reheating if necessary. To serve the soup, put a tablespoon of Pesto Sauce in the center and sprinkle with Parmesan cheese.

PER SERVING

Calories 331	Protein 10.6 grams	Carbohydrate 10.3 grams
Fiber 3 grams	Fat 27.6 grams	Net Carbs 7.3 grams

Lamb Stew

I love lamb. Give it to me roasted, grilled, broiled, sautéed, but in the winter give me stew—hot and slow! Everyone thinks Irish lamb stew is the best— not so. See how herbs give a decidedly Italian taste to this all-time favorite. Don't be put off by the anchovies—you won't taste fish in the finished dish, but if you leave them out, the stew will taste like something is missing.

1½   **pounds lamb stew meat, cut into 1-inch cubes**
    Salt to taste
    Freshly ground black pepper to taste
2   **tablespoons soy flour**
2   **tablespoons butter**
2   **tablespoons extra virgin olive oil**
1   **cup red wine**
1   **cup Chicken Stock** *(page 61)*
1   **pound white mushrooms, sliced ¼ inch thick**
1   **tablespoon chopped garlic**
1   **tablespoon chopped fresh rosemary**
    or 1 teaspoon dried rosemary
1   **teaspoon chopped fresh oregano**
    or a pinch of dried oregano
3   **2-inch strips lemon zest**
2   **anchovy fillets**
¼   **cup chopped fresh Italian parsley**

SERVES 4

Season the lamb with salt and pepper. Dust with flour and toss to coat. In a large heavy skillet, heat the butter and olive oil over moderately high heat and brown the lamb 2 to 3 minutes in batches without crowding the pan. As the lamb browns, transfer the cubes to a large heavy saucepan. Deglaze the skillet with wine, scraping up any brown bits and add this liquid to the lamb. Add stock, mushrooms, garlic, rosemary, oregano, zest, anchovies, and salt and pepper to taste. Bring the mixture to a boil, cover, reduce heat to low, and simmer for 45 minutes to 1 hour or until lamb is very tender. Remove lemon zest. Add parsley, and serve.

PER SERVING

Calories 490	Protein 48.5 grams	Carbohydrate 7.8 grams
Fiber 2 grams	Fat 25 grams	Net Carbs 5.8 grams

Beef Stew Abruzzi Style

The Abruzzi region of Italy is a mountainous area that lies between the Adriatic and the peaks of the Apennines. The food eaten there is quite hearty, and this stew is a fine example. The white wine from Abruzzi is Trebbiano.

1–1¼	pounds beef stew meat, cut into 1-inch cubes
	Salt to taste
	Freshly ground black pepper to taste
2	tablespoons soy flour
½	cup olive oil, divided
1	cup white wine
1	medium yellow onion, sliced
3	medium red bell peppers, cored, seeded, and sliced
2	cloves garlic, chopped
1	teaspoon red pepper flakes
1	15-ounce can whole peeled tomatoes, with juice, coarsely chopped
4	tablespoons chopped fresh Italian parsley, divided
1	bay leaf

SERVES 4

Season the beef with salt and pepper. Dust with soy flour and toss to coat. Heat ¼ cup of the olive oil in a large heavy skillet with a tight-fitting lid over moderately high heat. Brown the beef in batches, being careful not to overcrowd the skillet, then transfer to a dish. When all the beef is browned, add the wine and deglaze the skillet, scraping up any brown bits, and add this mixture to the beef. Set aside. Wash and dry the skillet. Add the remaining olive oil to the skillet and sauté the onion and bell peppers over moderate heat for 5 minutes. Add the garlic and red pepper flakes and sauté the mixture until the peppers are limp. Add the tomatoes, 2 tablespoons of the parsley, bay leaf, beef mixture, salt, and pepper. Reduce the heat to low, cover, and simmer until the beef is tender, about 1 hour. Remove bay leaf. Serve with the remaining parsley.

PER SERVING

Calories 502	Protein 22 grams	Carbohydrate 9 grams
Fiber 2.7 grams	Fat 43 grams	Net Carbs 6.3 grams

CHAPTER THREE

Salads, Sauces, and Dressings

INSALATA, SALSAS,
E CONDIMENTI

Pear Salad with Goat Cheese

Mixed Seafood Salad (INSALATA FRUTTI DI MARE)

Fennel and Orange Salad

Balsamic Vinaigrette

Mixed Herb Vinaigrette

Lemon Vinaigrette

Balsamic Onion Tomato Salad

Pesto Sauce

Green Sauce (SALSA VERDE)

White Sauce

Tomato Sauce

Roaster Red Bell Pepper Sauce

Squid and Cucumber Salad

Spinach and Shrimp Salad with Bacon and Egg

Pear Salad with Goat Cheese

This is an impressive-looking salad that is easy to prepare. The combination of hazelnuts and goat cheese offers a delicate crunch and mouth feel that you will love. Don't frown on using canned pears, because not only do they provide the right amount of sweetness, but they are also low in carbs (unlike their fresh counterparts).

1	4-ounce goat cheese log
¼	cup fresh hazelnuts, chopped and toasted *(see page 28)*
4	canned pear halves, packed in water
4	tablespoons fresh lemon juice
2	tablespoons butter
1	head frisée, washed, dried, and torn into bite-sized pieces
½	cup extra virgin olive oil
	Salt to taste
	Freshly ground black pepper

SERVES 4

Cut the goat cheese into ¼-inch slices and form into rounded pucks. Dredge goat cheese in hazelnuts, pressing the nuts into the cheese. Chill.

Cut pear halves lengthwise into ½-inch strips.

In a medium skillet, heat butter over moderately high heat. Add the goat cheese pucks and cook for 1 minute; turn and cook another minute, until browned. Transfer cheese to paper towels to drain.

In a salad bowl, toss the frisée with oil, remaining lemon juice, and salt and pepper to taste. Divide the mixture among four salad plates and garnish with pears and cheese.

.

PER SERVING

Calories 457	Protein 7.7 grams	Carbohydrate 11.6 grams
Fiber 4.4 grams	Fat 44 grams	Net Carbs 7.2 grams

Mixed Seafood Salad

INSALATA FRUTTI DI MARE

I have such fond memories of this dish and the evenings spent cooking it on the beach, and eating it with a group of friends. Use the absolute freshest seafood you can get for this dish, and you, too, will have some great memories. Don't skimp on the red pepper flakes, and be sure to cut the red onion into the thinnest of slices so as not to overpower the sweetness of each ingredient.

⅔ cup extra virgin olive oil, divided
1½ teaspoons minced garlic, divided
½ pound mussels, scrubbed and debearded
1 pound clams, scrubbed
½ pound prawns, peeled and deveined
½ pound halibut, cut into 1-inch pieces
6 ounces cleaned calamari, cut into rings
2 fresh plum tomatoes, chopped
½ medium red onion, sliced paper thin
2 stalks celery, finely chopped
¼ cup roughly chopped fresh Italian parsley
1 teaspoon red pepper flakes
Juice of 2 lemons
Salt to taste
Freshly ground black pepper

SERVES 4

In a large skillet with a lid, heat 2 tablespoons of the olive oil over moderate heat. Add ½ teaspoon of garlic, the mussels, and the clams and stir to combine. Cover and steam for 5 minutes, or until shells open; discard any unopened mussels or clams. Transfer shellfish to plate, and set aside until cool enough to handle. Wash and dry the skillet.

In the skillet, heat 2 tablespoons of olive oil over moderately high heat. Add ½ teaspoon garlic, the prawns, the halibut, and the calamari, and sauté for 5 minutes or until fish and shellfish are tender. Transfer the mixture to a bowl large enough to hold all the seafood. Set aside and cool to room temperature. Remove mussels and clams from shells and add them to the bowl. Stir to combine, cover, and chill.

In a bowl large enough to hold all the ingredients, combine tomatoes, remaining garlic, onion, celery, parsley, and pepper flakes. Add the seafood and toss together. Drizzle with remaining olive oil; then add lemon juice, salt, and pepper. Stir to combine, and chill before serving.

PER SERVING

Calories 638	Protein 53 grams	Carbohydrate 12.8 grams
Fiber 1.1 grams	Fat 41 grams	Net Carbs 11.7 grams

Fennel and Orange Salad

To direct a recipe in which each ingredient plays an equal role is a creative challenge, but I think I have succeeded in manipulating the supporting ingredients to accompany this low-carb taste sensation.

2   medium oranges
¼   small red onion, thinly sliced
1   large fennel bulb, quartered and thinly sliced,
         reserving leaves for garnish
2   teaspoons red wine vinegar
1   clove garlic, minced
     Salt to taste
     Freshly ground black pepper
1   medium head romaine lettuce
6   tablespoons extra virgin olive oil
2   ounces pecorino cheese, shaved

SERVES 6

Cut the peel and pith away from the oranges and discard. Using a sharp knife, carefully cut orange segments from the orange membranes. Put orange segments in a bowl and squeeze 2 tablespoons of juice from the membranes over them. Add onion, fennel, vinegar, garlic, salt, and pepper and toss until well combined.

Wash the romaine lettuce, dry thoroughly, tear into bite-sized pieces, and put in a salad bowl. Add orange and fennel mixture and toss. Drizzle with olive oil and toss again. Top with shaved cheese and fennel leaves.

PER SERVING

Calories 219	Protein 6.3 grams	Carbohydrate 12 grams
Fiber 4.3 grams	Fat 16.7 grams	Net Carbs 7.7 grams

Balsamic Vinaigrette

Balsamic vinegar is an essential ingredient in Italian cooking. Balsamic vinegar can be pricey with age—just like the women in my life. Inexpensive great-tasting balsamic vinegar is Colavita's from Modena. Unlike cider vinegar, balsamic vinegar is aged and its sweet taste adds a new dimension to salads and even fruit. It is also great as a brush-on for grilled vegetables. In this recipe I have modified a traditional vinaigrette with Dijon mustard. (I borrowed from the French since they borrowed freely from the Italians!)

5 tablespoons balsamic vinegar
1 tablespoon minced garlic
2 teaspoons Dijon mustard
Salt to taste
Freshly ground black pepper to taste
1 cup extra virgin olive oil

YIELDS APPROXIMATELY 1¼ CUPS

In a small bowl, whisk together the vinegar, garlic, mustard, salt, and pepper. Add the olive oil in a thin stream while whisking.

PER SERVING (2 TABLESPOONS)

Calories 198	Protein .15 grams	Carbohydrate 1.6 grams
Fiber .03 grams	Fat 22 grams	Net Carbs 1.6 grams

Mixed Herb Vinaigrette

This vinaigrette provides a great splash of taste that really perks up a dish. It's a great substitute for bottled Italian dressing. The Splenda substitution really brings down the carbs.

¼   cup white wine vinegar
1   tablespoon Dijon mustard
½   teaspoon Splenda granular
¼   teaspoon dried basil
    or ¾ teaspoon fresh chopped basil
¼   teaspoon dried oregano
    or ¾ teaspoon fresh chopped oregano
¼   teaspoon dried thyme
    or ¾ teaspoon fresh chopped thyme
    Salt to taste
    Freshly ground black pepper to taste
¾   cup extra virgin olive oil

YIELDS APPROXIMATELY 1 CUP

In a small bowl, whisk the vinegar, mustard, Splenda, basil, oregano, thyme, salt, and pepper. Whisking constantly, add the oil in a thin stream. Chill until ready to serve.

PER SERVING (2 TABLESPOONS)

Calories 206	Protein .14 grams	Carbohydrate 6.4 grams
Fiber .10 grams	Fat 20.4 grams	Net Carbs 6.3 grams

Lemon Vinaigrette

On the Greek Isle of Santorini at an outdoor taverna, I enjoyed a
wonderful lunch that consisted of lamb and a delicious lemon dressing.
I told the waiter (who happened to be the owner) that there must be
Sicilian lemons in his vinaigrette; he looked at me for a moment, then
with a big grin, said that his brother lived in Sicily and had sent him a
box of Sicilian lemons. Needless to say, the ouzo kept coming—on the house!
Great on grilled lamb and fish and drizzled on raw oysters and clams.

¼ cup fresh lemon juice
1 tablespoon minced fresh Italian parsley
Pinch of salt
Freshly ground black pepper to taste
¾ cup extra virgin olive oil

YIELDS APPROXIMATELY 1 CUP

In a small bowl, whisk together the lemon juice, parsley, salt, and pepper. Add the olive oil in a thin stream, whisking constantly. Chill until ready to serve.

PER SERVING (2 TABLESPOONS)

Calories 181	Protein .04 grams	Carbohydrate .7 grams
Fiber .05 grams	Fat 20 grams	New Carbs .6 grams

Balsamic Onion Tomato Salad

*After an exciting drive past the erupting Mt. Etna, and then following
a winding narrow pass up the mountain to Hotel Villa Ducale in Taormina,
I needed some food and wine (more so wine). On my arrival at the hotel, the
day manager, Enzo, said with Italian charm, "No problema! No problema!"
His perfect solution was this simple salad, along with great cheese and vino
—perfetto! And there in my room, from the safety of the hotel balcony,
I had a marvelous view of Mt. Etna's fireworks display. Make this
salad to enjoy as a light supper or lunch on a hot day.*

1   large red onion, chopped
4   fresh ripe plum tomatoes, coarsely chopped
1   rib celery, sliced thin
1   large clove garlic, minced
¼   teaspoon dried thyme or ½ teaspoon chopped fresh thyme
2   tablespoons fresh Italian parsley, chopped
    Salt to taste
    Freshly ground black pepper
    Serves 4
    Balsamic Vinaigrette *(page 73)*, Lemon Vinaigrette *(page 75)*,
      or Mixed Herb Vinaigrette *(page 74)*

SERVES 4

In a large bowl, toss the salad ingredients with the dressing.

PER SERVING

Calories 31	Protein 1.1 grams	Carbohydrate 6.8 grams
Fiber 1.6 grams	Fat .30 grams	Net Carbs 5.2 grams

Pesto Sauce

On a recent visit to Naples, Italy, I was delighted to see my favorite herb, basil, growing in pots on just about every neighborhood windowsill and balcony. It doesn't seem so long ago that this fragrant herb was available only during the summer months and only from the garden, but today you can find it year-round in any produce market or supermarket. I also keep some growing in a pot on a sunny windowsill so I can just pluck a few leaves to use when I need to add basil to a recipe. Basil (and this Pesto Sauce) is great on meats, on vegetables, in soups and stews, and also as a sandwich spread (on low-carb bread, of course).

2	cups loosely packed fresh basil leaves
2–3	cloves garlic
3	tablespoons pine nuts, toasted *(see page 28)*
½	cup extra virgin olive oil
½	cup Parmesan cheese
3	tablespoons butter
¼	teaspoon white pepper
	Salt to taste

YIELDS APPROXIMATELY 1¼ CUPS

Put half the basil in the bowl of a food processor and chop. Add the remaining basil along with the garlic and pine nuts and chop coarsely. With the motor running, drizzle the olive oil through the feed tube, stopping occasionally to scrape down the sides. Add the Parmesan cheese, butter, and pepper and process until well combined. Adjust seasoning with salt.

You can also freeze pesto for future use, storing it in an airtight container. Cover with a thin layer of olive oil. I like to freeze it in ice cube trays. Each cube equals 2 tablespoons.

PER SERVING (2 TABLESPOONS)

Calories 162	Protein 2.6 grams	Carbohydrate 1.2 grams
Fiber .48 grams	Fat 17 grams	Net Carbs .7 grams

Green Sauce

SALSA VERDE

This versatile sauce can be used as a dip for fresh and/or blanched vegetables and as a sauce for grilled meats and fish.

1	cup chopped fresh Italian parsley
¼	cup chopped scallions (in this recipe, the green portion)
2	anchovy fillets
1	tablespoon capers
1	tablespoon lemon zest
1	teaspoon chopped garlic
3	tablespoons freshly squeezed lemon juice
	Salt to taste
	Freshly ground black pepper to taste
¾–1	cup extra virgin olive oil

YIELDS APPROXIMATELY 1½ CUPS

In the bowl of a food processor, combine the parsley, scallions, anchovy fillets, capers, zest, and garlic, and blend or process until evenly chopped and well combined. Add lemon juice, salt, and pepper and mix again. With the motor running, add the olive oil in a thin stream, stopping the motor and scraping down the sides occasionally. Adjust seasoning with salt and pepper.

PER SERVING (2 TABLESPOONS)

Calories 145	Protein .43 grams	Carbohydrate 1 gram
Fiber .32 grams	Fat 16 grams	Net Carbs .7 grams

White Sauce

Since soy flour doesn't have the thickening power of white flour,
and cornstarch cannot be reheated (it breaks down), I've used a
little white flour to yield 2 cups of sauce.

2   tablespoons butter
1½ tablespoons flour
2   cups half-and-half
¼   teaspoon nutmeg to taste
     Salt to taste
     White pepper to taste

YIELDS APPROXIMATELY 2 CUPS

In a small saucepan, heat the butter over moderate heat until it just bubbles; be sure it doesn't brown. Whisk in the flour and cook for 60 seconds without browning. Slowly whisk the half-and-half into the sauce; add nutmeg, salt, pepper and simmer on low heat for 5 to 8 minutes, stirring constantly. The sauce should have the consistency of cream and no trace of a floury taste.

PER SERVING (2 TABLESPOONS)

Calories 56	Protein 1.1 grams	Carbohydrate 1.6 grams
Fiber .03 grams	Fat 4.5 grams	Net Carbs 1.6 grams

Tomato Sauce

One of my aunts was married to an Irishman, so she would add a green bell pepper in his honor, but he never knew it because she chopped it fine and it disappeared in the sauce. Kidding aside, I find the addition of green pepper helps to flavor the sauce.

¼   cup extra virgin olive oil
½   cup finely chopped onion
¼   cup finely chopped green bell pepper
¼   cup finely chopped celery
1   teaspoon chopped garlic
1   28-ounce can Italian plum tomatoes
     with their juice, coarsely chopped
½   teaspoon dried basil
     or 1½ teaspoons chopped fresh basil
¼   teaspoon dried oregano
     or 1½ teaspoons chopped fresh oregano
     Salt to taste
     Freshly ground black pepper to taste

YIELDS APPROXIMATELY 4 CUPS

In a medium saucepan, heat the olive oil over moderate heat and add the onion, bell pepper, celery, and garlic. Sauté until the onion is translucent, but not browned. Add the tomatoes, basil, oregano, salt, and pepper and bring just to a boil. Reduce the heat immediately to a simmer and cook, uncovered, for 30 minutes or until flavors have blended.

PER SERVING (½ CUP)

Calories 85	Protein 1.1 grams	Carbohydrate 6 grams
Fiber 1.4 grams	Fat 7 grams	Net Carbs 4.6 grams

Variation: For **MEAT SAUCE**, sauté extra-lean ground beef (I prefer a mix of beef and pork), about 1½ pounds total. Discard rendered fat, then add meat to sauce when ready to simmer for the last 30 minutes.

YIELDS APPROXIMATELY 6 CUPS

PER SERVING (½ CUP)

Calories 153	Protein 12.4 grams	Carbohydrate 3.9 grams
Fiber .9 grams	Fat 9.7 grams	Net Carbs 3 grams

Roasted Red Bell Pepper Sauce

This sauce can be used with grilled meat and seafood or as a dip for vegetables.

3	medium red bell peppers or 1½ cups drained commercially prepared roasted red peppers
½	cup toasted walnuts, ground fine *(see page 28)*
2	cloves garlic, chopped
1–2	tablespoons balsamic vinegar
1	tablespoon chopped fresh Italian parsley
¼	teaspoon red pepper flakes
1	teaspoon chopped fresh oregano or ½ teaspoon dried oregano
	Salt to taste
	Freshly ground black pepper to taste
6–8	tablespoons extra virgin olive oil

YIELDS 2 CUPS

If using fresh red peppers, preheat the broiler. Roast the peppers on a foil-lined baking sheet under the broiler, turning as the skin blisters, until evenly charred on all sides. Put the peppers in a bowl and cover with a clean towel or plastic wrap until cool enough to handle. Cut the peppers lengthwise and remove the stems, cores, and seeds. Peel and discard the charred skins.

In the bowl of a food processor, combine the peppers, walnuts, and garlic and process until fairly smooth. Add vinegar, parsley, pepper flakes, oregano, salt, and pepper and blend together. With the motor running, gradually add the olive oil in a thin stream until the sauce lightens in color and thickens slightly.

PER SERVING (2 TABLESPOONS)

Calories 85	Protein .81grams	Carbohydrate 2.3 grams
Fiber .72 grams	Fat 8.4 grams	Net Carbs 1.6 grams

Squid and Cucumber Salad

Squid is one of my favorite foods. Although it is excellent breaded and fried, there are numerous ways to prepare it—all equally delicious. Here it is naked, simply tossed with some flavorful ingredients for an elegant dish.

2   medium cucumbers, peeled and cubed
2   medium fresh ripe tomatoes, peeled, seeded, and chopped
½   cup extra virgin olive oil
     Juice of 2 lemons
¼   cup chopped fresh Italian parsley
     or 2 tablespoons dried parsley
1   clove garlic, minced
⅓   cup chopped fresh basil
1   pound cleaned squid, cut into bite-sized pieces
     with tentacles separate
     Salt to taste

SERVES 4 AS A MAIN COURSE
OR 6 AS AN APPETIZER

Bring a large pot of salted water to a boil. While the water is heating, combine the cucumbers, tomatoes, olive oil, lemon juice, parsley, garlic, and basil. Stir well to combine and set aside.

Add the squid pieces to the boiling water, reserving the tentacles, and cook until just tender, 30 to 60 seconds. Using a strainer, immediately scoop the squid from the water and set in a colander to drain. Add the tentacles and cook until just firm, about 30 seconds, and transfer to the colander to cool. When the squid is cool, add it to the cucumber mixture, season with salt, and toss. Serve immediately.

PER SERVING (MAIN COURSE)

Calories 377	Protein 19 grams	Carbohydrate 11.5 grams
Fiber 1.7 grams	Fat 29 grams	Net Carbs 9.8 grams

Spinach and Shrimp Salad with Bacon and Egg

On a sunny morning after a grand "love" night, make this for your partner. This will cap the memory. The ingredients should be ready in your refrigerator (think ahead), so that the scent of the pancetta frying in the morning will be a very welcome greeting, and the ingredients will nourish you. Of course, a glass of Prosecco will be in order.

1	tablespoon extra virgin olive oil
4	thin slices pancetta
1	10-ounce bag spinach leaves, trimmed, washed, and thoroughly dried
6	ounces cooked baby shrimp
½	cup red onion, thinly sliced
½	cup red bell pepper, thinly sliced
3	tablespoons Balsamic Vinaigrette *(page 73)*
2	hard boiled eggs, chopped

SERVES 4

In a small skillet, heat the olive oil over moderate heat. Add pancetta and cook until golden on both sides. Transfer to paper towels to drain.

To assemble the salad, put the spinach, shrimp, onion, and bell pepper in a large bowl and toss. Drizzle with vinaigrette and toss again. Divide the salad among four chilled salad plates. Sprinkle with the chopped egg and garnish each with a slice of pancetta.

PER SERVING

Calories 227	Protein 15 grams	Carbohydrate 6.3 grams
Fiber 2.7 grams	Fat 16 grams	Net Carbs 3.6 grams

CHAPTER FOUR

Vegetables

VERDURE E CONTORII

Eggplant Trapanese
Eggplant Rollatini
Eggplant with White Sauce
Marinated Eggplant and Bell Peppers
Cauliflower Siciliano
Cauliflower Gratin
Fried Cauliflower with Caper Aioli
Sautéed Broccoli
Broccoli with Mustard Sauce
Sautéed Spinach
Mushrooms Parsley, Garlic Style
Cabbage Frittata
Zucchini (Carpione) with a Dressing
Artichokes (Tegame) in the Pan
Grilled Asparagus, Green Beans, and Radicchio
Oven Roasted Vegetables
Sautéed Red Cabbage

Eggplant Trapanese

This dish originated in the port city of Trapani, Sicily. The unique flavor of the vinegar sauce as the final topping makes this dish special. As an added bonus, a cup of eggplant is only 8.2 carbs, something the Trapanese never even considered.

2	medium eggplants, about 1 pound each
	Soy flour for dusting
½–1	cup extra virgin olive oil
	Salt to taste
	Freshly ground black pepper to taste
2	cloves garlic, chopped
1	cup water
1	tablespoon tomato paste
1	teaspoon chopped fresh rosemary
	or a pinch of dried rosemary
1½	teaspoons white flour
4	tablespoons white wine vinegar

SERVES 6

Peel the eggplants and slice into thin slices lengthwise. Salt slices and put in a colander to drain for 30 minutes. Pat the slices dry and dust in soy flour, shaking off excess. Heat the oil in a large skillet over moderately high heat. Add the eggplant gently in batches, without crowding the pan, and fry until golden on both sides, transferring slices to paper towels to drain. Arrange on a warm platter and keep warm.

Drain all but 2 tablespoons of olive oil from the pan and add the garlic. Sauté until golden; then add the water, tomato paste, rosemary, salt, and pepper. Reduce the heat to low and simmer gently for 5 minutes. In a separate bowl, add the white flour to the vinegar, whisking until smooth; then add this mixture to the tomato sauce. Simmer for 2 to 3 minutes and pour over the eggplant. Let the eggplant rest a minute or two to absorb the sauce; then serve warm or at room temperature.

PER SERVING

Calories 237	Protein 1.8 grams	Carbohydrate 18.7 grams
Fiber 4 grams	Fat 18 grams	Net Carbs 14.7 grams

Eggplant Rollatini

This is a crowd pleaser and a great dish if prepared using the best-quality ingredients, but be sure to serve fresh. This is not a dish that works well as a leftover.

1¾ cups Tomato Sauce *(page 80)*
    Olive oil for frying
1 large eggplant, cut lengthwise
    into ¼-inch slices
    Soy flour for dusting
3 eggs, lightly beaten
2 cups whole milk ricotta
1 cup shredded whole milk mozzarella
½ cup grated Parmesan cheese,
    plus 2 tablespoons for sprinkling
2 tablespoons chopped fresh Italian parsley
2 tablespoons chopped fresh basil
    or 2 teaspoons dried basil
    Salt to taste
    Freshly ground black pepper
6 thin slices prosciutto

SERVES 4

Preheat the oven to 350°F. Oil a shallow baking dish and pour enough Tomato Sauce in the baking dish to cover the bottom.

In a large skillet over moderately high heat, pour enough oil to come ¼ inch up the sides. Dust the eggplant slices with soy flour, dip in egg. Fry the eggplant in batches, without crowding the pan, until golden on both sides. Transfer the slices to paper towels to drain. Set aside.

In a medium bowl, combine the ricotta, mozzarella, ½ cup Parmesan cheese, parsley, basil, salt, and pepper. Lay a slice of eggplant on the work surface and cover with a piece of prosciutto that covers about half of the slice. Spread some of the cheese filling over the prosciutto, then roll up the slice. Arrange the rolls seam-side down in the baking dish, nearly cover with Tomato Sauce, and sprinkle with the remaining 2 tablespoons of Parmesan cheese. Bake for 25 to 30 minutes or until bubbling and golden on top. Let the eggplant rest 10 minutes before serving.

PER SERVING

Calories 740	Protein 35 grams	Carbohydrate 23 grams
Fiber 6.5 grams	Fat 58 grams	Net Carbs 16.5 grams

Eggplant with White Sauce

I know you've had eggplant many different ways, but once your mouth experiences this eggplant lasagna, watch out! Even people who are not crazy about eggplant will love this combo: mushrooms and zucchinis flavored with prosciutto and the White Sauce. Buy the good cheese for this recipe because you'll be able to tell the difference between a great cheese like Parmigiano Reggiano *and the run-of-the-mill supermarket stuff in the finished dish.*

1   large eggplant, about 1 pound
     Olive oil for frying
1   teaspoon chopped garlic
½   cup finely chopped prosciutto
½   pound mushrooms, thinly sliced
2   small zucchinis, thinly sliced
2   tablespoons fresh Italian parsley
     Salt to taste
     Freshly ground black pepper
2   cups White Sauce *(page 79)*
½   cup grated Parmesan cheese

SERVES 4

Heat the oven to 350°F.

Peel and cut the eggplant crosswise into ½-inch slices. Heat the oil in a large skillet to the depth of ½ inch over moderately high heat to 350°F. Add the slices carefully, without crowding the pan, and fry in batches until golden on both sides. As the eggplant is done, transfer slices to paper towels to drain.

Drain excess oil away, leaving 2 tablespoons or so in the pan. Sauté the garlic and prosciutto until golden, then add the mushrooms and zucchinis and continue to sauté until the zucchinis are tender and beginning to color. Add the parsley, salt, and pepper and remove from heat.

Oil a baking dish. Cover the bottom of the dish with White Sauce, and arrange half the eggplant slices in a single layer on top of the sauce. Sprinkle with 1 tablespoon of the cheese. Spread half of the mushroom mixture over this and cover with ½ cup of sauce. Repeat a layer of eggplant and cheese, then a layer of the mushroom mixture, finishing with enough sauce to just cover the vegetables. Sprinkle with the remaining cheese and bake for 30 minutes. Let rest 10 minutes before serving.

PER SERVING

Calories 471	Protein 16 grams	Carbohydrate 18 grams
Fiber 4.4 grams	Fat 37 grams	New Carbs 13.6 grams

Marinated Eggplant and Bell Peppers

When I was a little guy and Mom packed me a sandwich for lunch, being Italian she also packed a side dish of marinated eggplant and bell peppers. Even back then I was creative with my meals, and I'd inevitably put the eggplant and peppers on my sandwich. A feast! (The olive oil used to drip through my brown paper lunch bag, and Mom could follow the drops to see if I went to school.)

1	large eggplant, peeled
½	cup extra virgin olive oil
2	medium yellow onions, thinly sliced
	Salt to taste
	Freshly cracked black pepper to taste
2	medium red bell peppers, cored, seeded, and cut into thin strips
1	clove garlic, chopped
¼	cup chopped fresh Italian parsley
¼	cup chopped fresh basil or 1 teaspoon dried basil

SERVES 4

Cut the eggplant in half lengthwise, then cut each piece in half cross-wise. Cut each piece into thin slices crosswise. Heat the olive oil in a large skillet over moderately high heat. Brown the eggplant in batches, being careful not to overcrowd the skillet. As the eggplant browns, transfer to paper towels to drain, then set aside.

In the same skillet, sauté the onions with salt and pepper over moderate heat about 5 minutes or until the onions are translucent. Add the bell peppers and sauté until caramelized, about 8 minutes more. Add the garlic and cook until golden. Transfer the mixture to a shallow serving dish. Add the sautéed eggplant, parsley, and basil and stir to combine. Let cool to room temperature before serving.

PER SERVING

Calories 273	Protein 3.5 grams	Carbohydrate 21.7 grams
Fiber 7.6 grams	Fat 21 grams	Net Carbs 14.1 grams

Cauliflower Siciliano

*Grandma used to make this dish, and as a child I wouldn't go near it.
Now you can't keep me away, because the flavors are bold and beautiful!
And don't worry about someone not liking anchovies, because they melt
into the olive oil and create the magic here.*

1	head cauliflower, cored and cut into small florets
½	cup olive oil
½	cup chopped onion
2	cloves garlic, minced
2	anchovy fillets, minced
¼	cup raisins
2	tablespoons grated Parmigiano Reggiano cheese
2	tablespoons soy flour
2	tablespoons chopped fresh Italian parsley
	Juice and zest of 1 lemon
	Salt to taste
	Freshly ground black pepper to taste

SERVES 4

Bring a large pot of salted water to a boil. Add the cauliflower and cook until just tender. With a slotted spoon, transfer to a serving bowl. Keep warm.

Heat the olive oil in a medium skillet and sauté the onion for 5 minutes. Add the garlic and anchovies and sauté until garlic is golden. Add the raisins, cheese, soy flour, and parsley; stir well. Add the mixture to the cauliflower, along with the lemon juice and zest. Season with salt and pepper and stir well to combine. Serve warm or chilled.

PER SERVING

Calories 353	Protein 7.2 grams	Carbohydrate 19 grams
Fiber 5 grams	Fat 30 grams	Net Carbs 14 grams

Cauliflower Gratin

*Since cauliflower is low in carbs (5.1 per cup cooked), it makes a
great satisfying side dish and, yes, the good Parmesan cheese and
White Sauce are better than macaroni and cheese.*

1   medium head of cauliflower, cored
      and cut into small florets
1½ cups White Sauce *(page 79)*
½   cup grated Parmesan cheese
4   tablespoons fresh Italian parsley, chopped, divided
     Salt to taste
     Freshly ground black pepper to taste

SERVES 4

Preheat the oven to 350°F. Butter a baking dish large enough to hold
all of the ingredients. Bring a large pot of salted water to a boil. Add
the cauliflower and cook until tender when pierced with a knife, but
not mushy. With a slotted spoon, transfer the cauliflower to a colander to drain. In a large bowl, combine the cauliflower, White Sauce,
Parmesan, and 2 tablespoons of the parsley. Toss until coated and season to taste with salt and pepper. Arrange the cauliflower mixture in
the baking dish and bake at 350°F for 20 minutes, or until the sauce is
bubbling. Sprinkle with the remaining 2 tablespoons of parsley and
serve.

PER SERVING

Calories 250	Protein 10.4 grams	Carbohydrate 12.8 grams
Fiber 3.8 grams	Fat 16.7 grams	Net Carbs 9 grams

Fried Cauliflower with Caper Aioli

When my Aunt Rosa would make this dish, she'd eat three-quarters of it before she got it to the dinner table. Good thing it's low in carbs. I've substituted soy for regular flour, and that lowers the carbs even more.

1   cup mayonnaise
1   tablespoon freshly squeezed lemon juice
1   tablespoon capers, chopped
1   clove garlic, minced
     Salt to taste
     Freshly ground black pepper to taste
     Olive oil for frying
     Soy flour for dusting
1   large head cauliflower, cored
        and cut into florets
3   eggs, beaten

SERVES 4

To make the aioli, combine the mayonnaise, lemon juice, capers, garlic, salt, and pepper in a small bowl, and stir well to combine. Set aside.

In a medium saucepan, heat enough oil to measure a depth of 2 inches to 350°F. Put the soy flour in a medium bowl and add a handful or two of the cauliflower florets. Toss to dust the cauliflower, then transfer to a sieve set over the bowl of soy flour. Shake off excess, letting it fall into the bowl. Dip the pieces in the beaten egg, and fry until golden brown, 3 to 5 minutes. Transfer to paper towels to drain, and keep warm while you fry the remaining pieces. When all the cauliflower is fried, season with salt and pepper and serve immediately with the aioli for dipping.

PER SERVING

Calories 628	Protein 9.6 grams	Carbohydrate 13.5 grams
Fiber 5.4 grams	Fat 61.8 grams	Net Carbs 8.1 grams

Sautéed Broccoli

*When I was a little guy, Mom would make rapini (Italian broccoli)
instead of regular broccoli—I grew to love it! It is true that rapini has
a somewhat bitter taste, but that's what allows this veggie to mate
so well with meat main courses like Italian sausages, pork roasts,
chops, et cetera. If you're not a fan of rapini, use regular broccoli.*

1	bunch broccoli or rapini, washed and stem-trimmed
¼	cup olive oil
2	cloves garlic, chopped
1	pinch red pepper flakes
	Salt to taste
½	cup water

SERVES 4

Starting at the stem end, cut the broccoli or rapini into pieces ½ inch
thick or, if you prefer, bite-size. In a medium skillet with a lid, heat the
olive oil over moderately high heat and add the garlic and red pepper
flakes. When the garlic is golden, add the broccoli and salt and sauté
until the broccoli begins to brown. Add the water, reduce heat to low,
and cover. Cook until tender and serve immediately.

Variation: Sautéed butcher-quality Italian pork sausages (hot or sweet)
would make this an ideal main course. Cooked sausages can be served
on the side or cooked and sliced and added to broccoli.

PER SERVING

Calories 138	Protein 1.8 grams	Carbohydrate 3.5 grams
Fiber 17 grams	Fat 13.7 grams	Net Carbs 13.5 grams

Broccoli with Mustard Sauce

*Broccoli is a very nutritious and versatile vegetable. It is low in carbs,
has antioxidant qualities, and is always available. Here I use it to create a tasty
side dish that provides an alternative to plain steamed broccoli.*

1	medium head broccoli
½	cup Chicken Stock *(page 61)*
4	tablespoons butter
2	cups half-and-half
4	tablespoons soy flour
2	teaspoons Dijon mustard
½	teaspoon ground dried thyme
	or 1½ teaspoons chopped fresh thyme
	Freshly ground pepper
	Salt to taste

SERVES 4

In a covered saucepan, steam broccoli in Chicken Stock. When cooked, remove broccoli. Add butter, half-and-half, and soy flour to pan. Mix in Dijon mustard, thyme, pepper, and salt. Cook until reduced. Return broccoli to pan to bathe in sauce. Serve hot.

PER SERVING

Calories 332	Protein 11 grams	Carbohydrate 14 grams
Fiber 5.2 grams	Fat 25.5 grams	Net Carbs 8.8 grams

Sautéed Spinach

*Sautéed spinach is a great side dish because it goes with any number of
entrees from meat to poultry to seafood. Although you can use frozen spinach,
I always try to use fresh, because the taste and consistency are always better.
If you like anchovies, add a couple of fillets to the oil for a great flavor boost.*

¼   cup olive oil
1   medium yellow onion, minced
2   stalks celery, minced
2   cloves garlic, minced
1¼ pounds spinach, washed
     Salt to taste
     Freshly ground black pepper to taste

SERVES 4

Heat the olive oil in a large skillet over moderately high heat and add
the onion. Sauté the onion until translucent; then add the celery and
garlic. Sauté until the celery is tender. Increase the heat and add the
spinach, salt, and pepper and sauté until the spinach is wilted. Serve
immediately.

PER SERVING

Calories 165	Protein 4.5 grams	Carbohydrate 8.1 grams
Fiber 4.5 grams	Fat 14 grams	Net Carbs 3.6 grams

Mushrooms Parsley, Garlic Style

*Today, there are such great varieties of exotic and hothouse mushrooms
at the greengrocer. Get your hands on some shiitakes, chanterelles,
and porcini mushrooms. Come on, don't be afraid to experiment. Try them,
you'll like 'em. (Mushrooms generally have 3–4 carbs per cup.)*

1 pound mixed wild or domestic white mushrooms,
   wiped clean and cut into ½-inch pieces
2 cloves garlic, chopped
½ teaspoon red pepper flakes
¼ cup olive oil
   Salt to taste
   Freshly ground black pepper
¼ cup chopped fresh Italian parsley

SERVES 4

In a skillet large enough to hold mushrooms without crowding, sauté
the garlic and pepper flakes in olive oil over moderately high heat
until aromatic. Add the mushrooms and sauté until golden. Add salt,
pepper, and parsley and stir 1 minute, then serve.

PER SERVING

Calories 152	Protein 3.5 grams	Carbohydrate 5.5 grams
Fiber 1.6 grams	Fat 14 grams	Net Carbs 3.9 grams

Cabbage Frittata

Cabbage in an Italian omelet is unusual, but it works well here with the combination of other ingredients. Eat it as a main meal or a side dish.

2   **tablespoons butter**
1½ **cups shredded napa or green cabbage**
½   **cup chopped scallions**
4   **eggs**
2   **tablespoons fresh Italian parsley, chopped**
1   **teaspoon Dijon mustard**
     Salt to taste
     Freshly ground black pepper
½   **cup coarsely grated fontina cheese**

SERVES 4 AS A SIDE DISH
OR 2 AS A MAIN COURSE

Preheat the broiler. In a medium nonstick, ovenproof skillet, add butter and sauté the cabbage and scallions 5 minutes, or until cabbage is wilted.

In a small bowl, combine eggs, parsley, mustard, salt, and pepper and whisk together.

Pour the mixture over the cabbage and stir gently to combine and cook over medium heat until the bottom is set. Sprinkle with cheese and put skillet under broiler. Cook until top is set and cheese is golden. Cut into wedges and serve.

PER SERVING (SIDE DISH)

Calories 194	Protein 10.6 grams	Carbohydrate 3.4 grams
Fiber 1 gram	Fat 15.5 grams	Net Carbs 2.4 grams

Zucchini (Carpione) with a Dressing

Carpione is a method of cooking fish (carp, actually) that is now used with vegetables when we drizzle the dressing over the finished dish. Someone added the egg along the way.

2	medium zucchinis
6	tablespoons olive oil
	Salt to taste
	Freshly ground black pepper
2	cloves garlic, chopped
4	eggs
½	teaspoon chopped fresh sage or one teaspoon dried
1	tablespoon white wine vinegar

SERVES 4

Trim the zucchini ends and cut in half crosswise, then cut ¼-thick slices lengthwise; set aside.

Heat ¼ cup of olive oil in a large skillet over moderately high heat. Fry the zucchini on both sides until lightly colored and translucent, adding salt and pepper to taste. Transfer to a platter, laying each piece flat.

If necessary, add enough additional olive oil to the skillet to measure 2 tablespoons. Add the garlic to the skillet and sauté until aromatic. Break the eggs one at a time and add to the skillet, keeping the yolks intact and leaving room between each. Fry the eggs sunny-side up, then arrange over the zucchini.

In a small bowl, whisk the sage, 2 tablespoons of olive oil, vinegar, salt, and pepper. Drizzle over the eggs and zucchini.

PER SERVING

Calories 285	Protein 7.5 grams	Carbohydrate 7 grams
Fiber 1.2 grams	Fat 25.7 grams	Net Carbs 5.8 grams

Artichokes (Tegame) in the Pan

Artichokes, from the Italian articiocco, *were actually introduced into the United States by the Spanish in the eighteenth century and not by the Italians. This is a tasty, light dish that can be served as an appetizer or side dish.*

2	pounds baby artichokes
1	tablespoon fresh mint, minced
3	cloves garlic, minced
	Salt to taste
	Freshly ground black pepper
½	cup extra virgin olive oil
1	cup water

SERVES 8

Preheat the oven to 350°F.

Remove the tough outer leaves from the artichokes and cut each artichoke in quarters. Arrange in a roasting pan cut-side up, and press the mint and garlic into the leaves. Season with salt and pepper and drizzle with olive oil. Pour a cup or so of water over the chokes and bake uncovered until tender, about 30 minutes.

PER SERVING

| Calories 174 | Protein 3.8 grams | Carbohydrate 12.3 grams |
| Fiber 6.2 grams | Fat 13.7 grams | Net Carbs 6.1 grams |

Grilled Asparagus, Green Beans, and Radicchio

I am always searching for new grill ideas and this one I've recently debuted on television and it was a big hit. Remember though, it's easier to work with thick asparagus than the thin spears. If you can't get pancetta, substitute prosciutto.

20   thick asparagus spears, trimmed
¼   pound green beans, trimmed
    Salt to taste
    Freshly ground black pepper
4   tablespoons extra virgin olive oil
1   small head radicchio (round variety)
4   thin slices pancetta
    Juice and zest of 1 lemon
2   tablespoons balsamic vinegar
1   teaspoon chopped fresh thyme
    or a pinch of dried thyme

SERVES 4

Preheat the grill. Toss the asparagus and green beans in a mixing bowl with a pinch of salt and pepper. Coat with 2 tablespoons of the olive oil and set aside.

Cut the radicchio into quarters through the core. Wrap each quarter with a piece of pancetta. Season with salt and pepper; drizzle with 1 tablespoon of olive oil and set aside.

Brush the grill with olive oil. Put the radicchio, asparagus, and green beans on the grill. Grill, turning frequently, until the vegetables are golden brown and slightly blistered. Arrange on a platter and drizzle with the remaining olive oil, lemon juice, and balsamic vinegar. Sprinkle with zest and thyme.

PER SERVING

Calories 178	Protein 3.9 grams	Carbohydrate 10 grams
Fiber 3.3 grams	Fat 15 grams	Net Carbs 6.7 grams

Oven Roasted Vegetables

Depending on your main dish, you could season here with your own choice of flavors; for example, add oregano or thyme if your main course is meat. Perhaps sage or dill if your main course is fish.

¼   cup extra virgin olive oil
      Salt to taste
      Freshly ground black pepper
1   medium zucchini, sliced lengthwise into ¼-inch strips
¼   pound green beans, trimmed
2   fresh plum tomatoes, quartered lengthwise
1   medium red potato, cut into ⅛-inch slices
1   medium yellow bell pepper, cored,
      seeded, and cut lengthwise into 8 pieces
3 t ablespoons fresh Italian parsley, roughly chopped

SERVES 4

Preheat the oven to 400°F.

Cut a piece of baking parchment to fit a baking sheet. Oil the parchment lightly with olive oil and sprinkle with salt and pepper. Arrange the sliced vegetables flat on the seasoned pan and lightly brush the tops with olive oil. Sprinkle with salt and pepper.

Bake the vegetables for 30 minutes, or until they develop a light golden color. Stack on a dish and sprinkle with parsley.

PER SERVING

Calories 304	Protein 2.6 grams	Carbohydrate 14.7 grams
Fiber 2.8 grams	Fat 27.4 grams	Net Carbs 11.9 grams

Sautéed Red Cabbage

I've been trying to remember who gave me this recipe—was it Olga, my German friend who was married to an Italian innkeeper in the Swiss Alps, or was it Lina from Venice, who was married to a "crazy gondolier"? Well whatever, it's a great dish. I've just modified the recipe by using Splenda.

2	tablespoons extra virgin olive oil
1	small head red cabbage, thinly shredded
2	cloves garlic, crushed
1	medium yellow onion, sliced thin
¼	teaspoon ground coriander
1½	tablespoons red wine vinegar
2	tablespoons golden raisins
1	packet Splenda
	Salt to taste
	Freshly ground pepper

SERVES 4

In a large skillet, heat olive oil and add cabbage, garlic, and onion. Start with high heat, then reduce to moderate; add coriander, vinegar, raisins, Splenda, salt, and pepper. Cook until desired degree of doneness.

PER SERVING

Calories 130	Protein 2.5 grams	Carbohydrate 16.3 grams
Fiber 3.7 grams	Fat 7.2 grams	Net Carbs 12.3 grams

CHAPTER FIVE

Fish

P E S C E

Tuna with Onions and Mint
Tuna Tartare
Fried Squid with Deep-Fried Parsley
Sautéed Squid
Halibut Puttanesca
Halibut with Saffron Sauce
Baked Snapper with Bell Peppers and Onions
Snapper with Eggplant and Onions
Snapper Livornese
Shrimp with Peppers in Cream Wine Sauce
Shrimp with Fennel
Shrimp Milanese
Oven Roasted Salmon with Salsa Verde
Grilled Marinated Salmon
Sole Piccata
Sole Stuffed with Crabmeat
Marinated Grilled Swordfish
Pesce (Fish) with Artichoke Hearts
Roasted Trout with Herbs and Fennel
Scallops Marinara
Mussels with Tomato Sauce
Anchovy Peppers

Tuna with Onions and Mint

I stopped in Agrigento, Sicily, when the local restaurant was just about to close, but the owner's wife took pity on me and a hungry U.S. serviceman I had befriended, and made us this great dish. Combining mint, honey, and balsamic vinegar is probably a first for you, but when you taste this recipe you will e-mail me love notes!

4	tablespoons olive oil
2	medium yellow onions, thinly sliced
	Salt to taste
	Freshly ground black pepper to taste
4	tuna steaks, cut ¾ inch thick and 6–8 ounces each
¼	cup balsamic vinegar
¼	cup white wine
2	tablespoons chopped fresh mint
1	tablespoon honey

SERVES 4

Heat 3 tablespoons of the olive oil in a large skillet with a lid over moderate heat. Add the onions, salt, and pepper and sauté until the onions are softened, about 5 to 8 minutes. Cover loosely with a piece of foil and reduce the heat to moderately low. Cook, stirring occasionally, for 15 minutes, or until the onions are tender and caramelized. Transfer the onions along with any browned bits to a plate with a slotted spoon. If necessary, add another tablespoon of olive oil to the skillet and increase the heat to high. When the oil is hot, add the tuna and brown on one side, about 2 minutes. Turn the tuna over and add the onions, vinegar, wine, mint, honey, salt, and pepper. Heat through, then reduce the heat to moderately low, cover, and cook 2 to 3 minutes.

PER SERVING

Calories 462	Protein 47 grams	Carbohydrate 11.7 grams
Fiber 1 gram	Fat 23.4 grams	Net Carbs 10.7 grams

Tuna Tartare

*The tuna used in this recipe must be sashimi quality, bought from
a reputable fish market. Be sure, too, to know the tastes of
your guests before you try to serve them raw fish.*

1   pound ahi tuna
¼   cup minced red onion
1   tablespoon minced fresh Italian parsley
2   teaspoons chopped capers
     Juice and zest of 1 lemon
¼   cup extra virgin olive oil
     Salt to taste
     Freshly ground black pepper
6   ounces baby greens, washed and
        thoroughly dried

SERVES 4

Chop the tuna into small dice, then put in the bowl of a food processor. Pulse two or three times until evenly minced. Wrap the tuna
tightly in plastic and chill.

In a bowl, combine the chilled tuna with the onion, parsley,
capers, and zest. Stir well to combine. Drizzle with olive oil and
lemon juice and season with salt and pepper. Divide the greens among
four chilled salad plates and top with tuna tartare. Serve immediately.

PER SERVING

Calories 298	Protein 27 grams	Carbohydrate 3.7 grams
Fiber 1.3 grams	Fat 19.2 grams	Net Carbs 2.4 grams

Fried Squid with Deep-Fried Parsley

I've done this same recipe with cilantro when I'm doing a Latino taste or a diversion.
The soy flour in this recipe actually gives the squid a lighter flavor. Deep-fried parsley
is a great garnish for many dishes; don't be afraid to use it when the mood strikes.
Be sure your parsley is the flat-leafed Italian or European version only.

1½	pounds cleaned squid
	Olive oil for frying
	Soy flour for dusting
1	small bunch fresh Italian parsley
	Salt to taste
	Freshly ground black pepper to taste
2	lemons, cut into wedges

SERVES 4 AS A MAIN COURSE
OR 8 AS AN APPETIZER

Remove the tentacles from the squid and set aside. Cut the squid tubes into ¼-inch rings. In a medium saucepan, heat enough oil to measure 2 inches in depth to 350°F. Put soy flour in a medium bowl and add a handful or two of the squid rings. Toss to coat; then transfer the squid to a sieve held over the bowl of soy flour. Shake excess flour through sieve. Carefully add the squid to the hot oil, without overcrowding the pan. Fry the squid until golden brown, 3 to 4 minutes, and transfer to paper towels to drain. Keep the finished squid warm while you dust and fry the remaining tubes. Fry the tentacles in the same fashion and keep warm.

Fry the parsley sprigs in batches and drain on paper towels. Mound the squid on a warmed serving platter with the tentacles on top. Sprinkle with salt and pepper. Garnish the squid with the fried parsley and lemon wedges and serve immediately.

PER SERVING (MAIN COURSE)

Calories 286	Protein 27.3 grams	Carbohydrate 7 grams
Fiber 1 gram	Fat 16 grams	Net Carbs 6 grams

Sautéed Squid

Please, please, please pay attention when you're cooking squid, because it is too easy to overcook it. Overcooked squid is not good; it is a rubber band—so pay attention! Don't answer the phone or watch TV when you're cooking it.

2	tablespoons olive oil
2	cloves garlic, sliced
	Pinch of red pepper flakes
1	pound cleaned calamari, cut into strips
½	cup white wine
3	fresh plum tomatoes, diced
	Salt to taste
	Freshly ground black pepper to taste
¼	cup chopped fresh Italian parsley

SERVES 4 OR 6 AS AN APPETIZER

In a large skillet, heat the olive oil over moderately high heat, then add the garlic and pepper flakes. Cook until the garlic is golden; then add the squid and sauté for 1 minute. Add in the wine, tomatoes, salt, and pepper. Cook over moderate heat until heated through. Garnish with the parsley and serve.

PER SERVING (SERVING 4)

Calories 198	Protein 18.3 grams	Carbohydrate 6.6 grams
Fiber .67 grams	Fat 8.5 grams	Net Carbs 6 grams

Halibut Puttanesca

*While on an Alaskan cruise, I had the great opportunity to indulge in wild salmon
and halibut, indigenous to the area. One night, after having broiled fish
every night, I convinced the chef to serve it to me with puttanesca, my favorite
Italian sauce, and yes, I also ate it with a bit of al dente linguine. Enjoy!*

4	halibut fillets or steaks, about 8 ounces each
¼	cup olive oil
	Salt to taste
	Freshly ground black pepper to taste
2	cloves garlic, minced
¾	cup pitted, sliced calamata olives
½	medium yellow onion, sliced
¼	cup capers
2	fresh plum tomatoes, diced
2	tablespoons chopped fresh Italian parsley
¾ cup white wine	

SERVES 4

Preheat the oven to 400°F. Arrange the halibut on a parchment-lined
baking sheet. Drizzle both sides of the fish with olive oil, then season
with salt and pepper. Rub with garlic. Sprinkle each fillet with some
of the olives, onion, capers, tomatoes, and parsley. Drizzle each piece
of fish with white wine and bake in the oven for 10 minutes or until
the halibut is no longer translucent. Serve immediately.

PER SERVING

Calories 445	Protein 48 grams	Carbohydrate 5.6 grams
Fiber 1.8 grams	Fat 21.6 grams	Net Carbs 3.8 grams

Halibut with Saffron Sauce

*The Saffron Sauce brings out the best in this delicate white fish.
You'll think you're dining at the finest five-star kitchen—your own!*

4	halibut fillets or steaks, about 8 ounces each
½	cup olive oil, divided
	Salt to taste
	White pepper to taste
2	tablespoons butter
1	shallot, minced
1	clove garlic, minced
	Pinch of saffron
½	cup white wine
½	cup Fish Stock *(page 62)*
1	cup heavy cream

SERVES 4

Rub the fillets with ¼ cup of the olive oil and sprinkle with salt and pepper. Chill the fillets while you make the sauce.

In a saucepan, melt the butter over moderate heat and sauté the shallot until translucent. Add the garlic and saffron and cook for 3 minutes. Increase the heat and deglaze the pan with the wine, then add the Fish Stock. Reduce the liquid by half and add the cream.

Thicken the sauce until it coats the back of a spoon. Adjust the seasoning with salt and pepper and set aside in a warm place.

Heat the remaining olive oil in a large nonstick skillet over moderately high heat. Slide the fillets into the skillet, leaving room between each piece. Sear the fish until golden brown, 3 to 5 minutes. Turn the fillets over and cook another 3 to 5 minutes or until the halibut is no longer translucent. Serve immediately, drizzled with the saffron sauce.

PER SERVING

Calories 534	Protein 49.3 grams	Carbohydrate 2.6 grams
Fiber .03 grams	Fat 33.2 grams	Net Carbs 2.6 grams

Baked Snapper with Bell Peppers and Onions

I enjoyed this dish at the Hotel Savoy in Florence. Its preparation and ingredients were top-notch. Although green peppers have about 3 less carbs than red peppers do, I prefer the red—it seems they are easier for me to digest, and maybe for you, too.

½ cup olive oil
2 medium red bell peppers, cored,
    seeded, and sliced thin
2 medium yellow bell peppers, cored,
    seeded, and sliced thin
1 medium red onion, quartered
    Salt to taste
    Freshly ground black pepper to taste
2 cloves garlic, chopped
2 tablespoons chopped fresh Italian parsley
1 teaspoon chopped fresh oregano
    or ⅓ teaspoon dried oregano
4 red snapper fillets, about 8 ounces each
1 cup white wine

SERVES 4

Preheat the oven to 400°F. In a large skillet, heat the olive oil over moderate heat and add the bell peppers and red onion. Season with salt and pepper and sauté the vegetables until the peppers soften and collapse. Add the garlic, parsley, and oregano and stir to combine. Remove from heat and set aside.

Oil a baking dish large enough to hold the snapper fillets in one layer. Arrange the fillets in the dish and season with salt and pepper. Drizzle the fish with the wine, cover with foil, and bake in the oven for 10 to 12 minutes or until the snapper is no longer translucent.

Arrange veggies on each serving plate and place a snapper fillet in the center of each.

PER SERVING

Calories 480	Protein 33 grams	Carbohydrate 11.7 grams
Fiber 2.4 grams	Fat 29.4 grams	Net Carbs 9.3 grams

Snapper with Eggplant and Onions

A great fish restaurant in the resort town of Termoli presented this dish to our tour group of sixteen bon vivants. "Wow!" was the unanimous response.

6	tablespoons extra virgin olive oil, divided
1	medium eggplant, cut into ¾-inch cubes
1	medium yellow onion, sliced
2	cloves garlic, minced
½	cup white wine
¼	cup chopped fresh Italian parsley
¼	teaspoon red pepper flakes
	Salt to taste
	Freshly ground black pepper to taste
4	small red snapper fillets, about 6 ounces each

SERVES 4

Preheat the oven to 350°F.

In a large skillet, heat half of the olive oil over moderately high heat. Add the eggplant in batches and sauté the eggplant until golden brown on all sides. Transfer to paper towels to drain, and set aside. If necessary, add the remaining olive oil and reduce heat to medium. Sauté the onion until translucent, about 5 minutes. Add the garlic and cook until golden. Add the white wine, parsley, red pepper flakes, salt, and pepper. Return the eggplant to the skillet and stir to combine well and reheat. Arrange the snapper fillets on a parchment-lined baking sheet and cover each fillet with a quarter of the eggplant mixture. Bake for 10 minutes or until the flesh of the snapper is opaque throughout.

PER SERVING

Calories 364	Protein 25.5 grams	Carbohydrate 11.7 grams
Fiber 4.1 grams	Fat 22 grams	Net Carbs 7.6 grams

Snapper Livornese

This is one of those Italian recipes that get their name because the chef who created this blend of ingredients was from Livorna, a town south of Pisa. You'll find this dish listed on most Italian menus because it's so good. Capers are buds from a caper bush originally grown in southern Europe and now also grown in the United States and sold vinaigretted or salted. My secret is to rinse them before using. Here they make the dish. Capers add flavor and magic to many dishes; be creative, experiment—you can't make a mistake.

3	tablespoons extra virgin olive oil
½	cup chopped yellow onion
2	garlic cloves, chopped
½	pound white mushrooms, sliced
3	plum tomatoes, seeded and chopped
½	cup white wine
¼	cup pitted and halved calamata olives
2	tablespoons chopped fresh basil
	or 2 teaspoons dried basil
1	tablespoon capers
1	teaspoon chopped fresh oregano
	or a pinch of dried oregano
¼	teaspoon red pepper flakes
	Salt to taste
	Freshly ground black pepper to taste
4	red snapper fillets, 6–8 ounces each
¼	cup chopped fresh Italian parsley
	Lemon wedges for squeezing

SERVES 4

In a large skillet, heat the olive oil and sauté the onion and garlic for 5 minutes over moderate heat. Add the mushrooms, tomatoes, wine, olives, basil, capers, oregano, pepper flakes, salt, and pepper and stir well to combine. Bring the mixture to a boil; then reduce the heat to low and simmer uncovered for 10 minutes.

Push the mixture to one side of the skillet and lay the fillets skin-side down in the skillet. Mound the tomato mixture on top of the fillets, cover the skillet, and simmer for 8 to 10 minutes or until the fillets are firm and opaque. Sprinkle with parsley and serve with lemon wedges on the side.

PER SERVING

| Calories 289 | Protein 30 grams | Carbohydrate 8 grams |
| Fiber 2.1 grams | Fat 13.3 grams | Net Carbs 5.9 grams |

Shrimp with Peppers in Cream Wine Sauce

Dried porcini mushrooms have an intense flavor that makes this sauce come alive. You will love this dish.

½ ounce dried porcini mushrooms
¼ cup warm water
2 tablespoons butter
2 tablespoons extra virgin olive oil
½ cup minced onion
2 tablespoons minced shallots
2 teaspoons minced garlic
1 large red bell pepper, cored, seeded, and cut into thin strips
1 large green bell pepper, cored, seeded, and cut into thin strips
Salt to taste
Freshly ground black pepper to taste
½ cup white wine
1 cup heavy cream
1½ pounds shrimp, peeled and deveined
2 tablespoons chopped fresh Italian parsley
Grated Parmesan cheese

SERVES 4

In a small bowl combine the mushrooms and water. Set aside to soak for 20 minutes.

In a large skillet, heat the butter and olive oil over moderate heat and add the onion, shallots, and garlic. Sauté until the vegetables are soft, about 8 minutes. Add the bell peppers, mushrooms and their liquid, salt, and pepper and sauté until the peppers are softened but not cooked through. Increase the heat to moderately high; add the wine and cream and reduce to thicken. Reduce the heat slightly and add the shrimp, simmering until they are firm and pink, 3 to 5 minutes—do not over-cook. Add the parsley and serve with Parmesan on the side.

PER SERVING

Calories 565	Protein 38.2 grams	Carbohydrate 13.6 grams
Fiber 2.6 grams	Fat 37.8 grams	Net Carbs 11 grams

Shrimp with Fennel

*Liqueurs and wines were crafted by the monks way back in medieval times, and
their popularity in the culinary arts has evolved significantly over the centuries.
For nearly 1,300 years the most successful vineyards were owned and operated by
religious orders. Here, an already delicious dish is turned into a "divine intervention"
with a licorice-flavored liqueur such as sambuca or anisette. Heavenly!*

2	tablespoons butter
2	tablespoons oil
2	garlic cloves, chopped
⅓	cup chopped shallots
½	teaspoon fennel seeds
1	medium fennel bulb, cored and thinly sliced (reserve some leaves for garnish)
2	chopped scallions
	Salt to taste
	Freshly ground black pepper to taste
2	tablespoons anise liqueur such as sambuca, pernod, or anisette
½	cup white wine
½	cup clam juice
1½	pounds shrimp, peeled and deveined
1	fresh plum tomato, seeded and finely chopped

SERVES 4

Heat the butter and oil in a large skillet over moderate heat. Add the garlic and sauté until golden. Add the shallots and fennel seeds and sauté until the shallots are tender. Add the fennel, scallions, salt, and pepper and toss well. Cover loosely and steam 3 to 5 minutes or until the fennel is nearly tender, then uncover and let any excess liquid evaporate.

Averting your face, add the liqueur and ignite with a long match. Swirl the pan slightly until the flames die out; then add the wine and reduce by half. Add the clam juice, bring to a simmer, and drop the shrimp and tomatoes into the liquid. Simmer until the shrimp are firm and pink, 3 to 5 minutes. Serve immediately, garnished with coarsely chopped fennel leaves.

PER SERVING

Calories 371	Protein 36.1 grams	Carbohydrate 13 grams
Fiber 2.3 grams	Fat 15.7 grams	Net Carbs 10.7 grams

Shrimp Milanese

Italian foods do not generally mix cheese with fish, but to deliver a tasty, low-carb dish, I've used a shrimp coating of soy flour and cheese, which works exceptionally well. Of course, you know by now not to overcook the shrimp.

18   jumbo shrimp, shelled, deveined, and butterflied
2   tablespoons grated Parmigiano Reggiano cheese
2   tablespoons soy flour
    Dash white pepper
    Dash paprika
2   egg whites
    Olive oil for frying
    Lemon wedges

SERVES 2 AS A MAIN DISH
OR 4 AS AN APPETIZER

Butterfly the shrimp by cutting lengthwise (not all the way). Mix cheese, soy flour, white pepper, and paprika. Dip the shrimp into egg whites, then into cheese–soy flour mix.

In a medium skillet heat the oil and sauté shrimp lightly until opaque. Serve with lemon wedges.

PER SERVING (MAIN DISH)

Calories 271	Protein 24.7 grams	Carbohydrate 3 grams
Fiber .51 grams	Fat 17.6 grams	Net Carbs 2.5 grams

Oven Roasted Salmon with Salsa Verde

Salsa Verde is my favorite sauce to serve with salmon. I once prepared this dish for a popular Italian opera star, and he's never stopped singing its praises. Sorry I can't give you his name; if I do, I'll never get tickets to La Scala again.

	2-pound whole salmon fillet
¼	**cup extra virgin olive oil**
1	**teaspoon dried rosemary or**
	1 tablespoon chopped fresh rosemary
1	**teaspoon dried sage or**
	1 tablespoon chopped fresh sage
1	**teaspoon dried thyme or**
	1 tablespoon chopped fresh thyme
4	**thin slices lemon**
	Salt to taste
	Freshly ground black pepper to taste
½	**cup Salsa Verde** (*page 78*)

SERVES 4

Preheat the oven to 425°F.

Line a baking sheet with parchment. Lay the fillet on the parchment, skin-side down. Drizzle the salmon with the olive oil, then sprinkle with rosemary, sage, thyme, salt, and pepper. Rub the mixture gently into the salmon. Top with lemon slices and roast 25 to 30 minutes or until the flesh is light pink in the center. Transfer the fillet to a warm platter and serve with dollops of Salsa Verde.

PER SERVING

Calories 802	Protein 45.7 grams	Carbohydrate 1.7 grams
Fiber .75 grams	Fat 67.6 grams	Net Carbs 1 gram

Grilled Marinated Salmon

*Whether your salmon is wild or farm raised, you will enjoy the taste
of this healthy fish infused with this Italian marinade.*

½   cup minced yellow onion
3   tablespoons olive oil
2   teaspoons minced fresh rosemary
      or ¾ teaspoon dried rosemary
1   clove garlic, minced
1   teaspoon red pepper flakes
      Salt to taste
      Freshly ground black pepper to taste
4   salmon fillets, about 6 ounces each
2   tablespoons freshly squeezed lemon juice
2   teaspoons white wine vinegar
2   tablespoons chopped fresh Italian parsley

SERVES 4

In a small bowl combine the onion, olive oil, rosemary, garlic, pepper
flakes, salt, and pepper. Arrange the fillets in a shallow nonreactive
dish. Rub the marinade mixture over the entire surface of the fillets,
cover with plastic, and refrigerate at least 30 minutes.

Preheat the grill. When it is hot, put the fillets on skin-side up and
grill for 5 minutes. Turn the fillets over and grill 3 to 6 minutes more
or until the flesh is light pink throughout. Transfer to a warm platter
and drizzle with lemon juice and vinegar. Sprinkle with the parsley.

PER SERVING

Calories 422	Protein 334.3 grams	Carbohydrate 5.1 grams
Fiber .65 grams	Fat 28.7 grams	Net Carbs 4.5 grams

Sole Piccata

*You've probably eaten chicken or veal piccata, now experience the delicate,
exquisite taste of Sole Piccata, with the tang of capers and lemon and
the fragrance of garlic (also known as the Italian birth control pill).
(NOTE: When you get to the meat and poultry chapters, enjoy the Chicken
or Lamb Piccata, which has slightly different ingredients.)*

1¼   **pounds sole fillets**
    Salt to taste
    Freshly ground black pepper to taste
    Soy flour for dusting
¼   **cup olive oil**
2   **tablespoons butter**
1   **tablespoon minced shallots**
1   **clove garlic, minced**
½   **cup white wine**
2   **tablespoons capers**
2   **tablespoons lemon juice**
1   **tablespoon chopped fresh Italian parsley,
    plus 4 sprigs**

SERVES 4

Season the fillets with salt and pepper. Dust lightly with the soy flour.
In a large skillet, heat the olive oil over moderately high heat; add the
fillets slowly in batches without crowding the skillet. When the fillets
are lightly browned on one side, turn them over and brown the other
side. Transfer to a warmed platter, but do not stack the fillets on top
of each other. Keep the fillets warm while you make the sauce.

In the same skillet, heat the butter, shallots, and garlic. Sauté until
golden; then deglaze the skillet with the wine, scraping up any bits.
Add the capers, lemon juice, and chopped parsley and heat through,
reducing slightly. Pour the sauce over the fish and serve garnished
with the parsley.

PER SERVING

Calories 311	Protein 24 grams	Carbohydrate 1.8 grams
Fiber .23 grams	Fat 21 grams	Net Carbs 1.6 grams

Sole Stuffed with Crabmeat

*Although sole is technically any variety of flat fish from the Soleidae family,
today the nomenclature is not adhered to and other species are called "sole."
Whatever mild-flavored white-fleshed fish is available and affordable at your
fishmonger's will be enhanced with this combination of flavors.*

1   cup lump crabmeat
1   small red bell pepper, seeded and diced
2   tablespoons extra virgin olive oil
      (plus extra for brushing)
1   tablespoon capers, chopped
1   tablespoon chopped garlic
1   tablespoon pine nuts, toasted *(see page 28)*
¼   teaspoon white pepper
1   tablespoon fresh lemon juice
    Salt to taste
4   6-ounce sole fillets
1¼ cups Half-and-half

SERVES 4

Preheat the over to 350°F.

Mix crabmeat, bell pepper, olive oil, capers, garlic, pine nuts, pepper, lemon juice, and salt.

Lay fillets in a greased oven casserole (most attractive side down). Divide and spread stuffing on top of fillets, then roll up; put seam-side down, and fasten with wood picks, if needed. Brush with olive oil.

Pour approximately ½ inch of half-and-half into the casserole, and bake about 25 to 35 minutes.

PER SERVING

Calories 396	Protein 38.2 grams	Carbohydrate 5.7 grams
Fiber .63 grams	Fat 19.2 grams	Net Carbs 5.1 grams

Marinated Grilled Swordfish

*Swordfish is a great fish to cook. It also has the ability to absorb
the flavor of the ingredients it's cooked in and somehow blend
them in a way that is magic to the tongue.*

¼ cup freshly squeezed lemon juice
¼ cup chopped fresh Italian parsley
2 tablespoons capers
1 tablespoon chopped fresh oregano
   or 1 teaspoon dried oregano
3 cloves garlic
2 teaspoons lemon zest
   Salt to taste
   Freshly ground black pepper to taste
¾ cup extra virgin olive oil
4 swordfish steaks, cut ¾ inch thick

SERVES 4

In a food processor, combine the lemon juice, parsley, capers,
oregano, garlic, zest, salt, and pepper and blend until fairly smooth.
With the motor running, gradually drizzle in the olive oil, stopping
the motor to scrape down the sides of the work bowl occasionally.

Put the swordfish steaks in a glass or stainless steel dish and pour
three-quarters of the marinade over them, turning them to coat. Set
the remaining marinade aside. Let the fish marinate 30 minutes while
you preheat the grill.

Lightly oil the grill and cook the swordfish for 5 minutes; turn
and cook another 3 to 5 minutes or until swordfish is firm and opaque.
Serve the steaks immediately with the remaining marinade poured
over them.

PER SERVING

Calories 350	Protein 31 grams	Carbohydrate 1.2 grams
Fiber .21 grams	Fat 24 grams	Net Carbs 1 gram

Pesce (Fish) with Artichoke Hearts

I discovered this amazing dish at a popular fish restaurant in Rome (I had to make the dinner reservation two months in advance). The artichokes eaten in Italy were fresh, but I used frozen ones at home and they worked out nicely.

4   fish fillets, such as scrod, cod, or halibut
    Salt and pepper to taste
    Soy flour for dusting
4   tablespoons olive oil
½   cup white wine
9   ounces frozen artichoke hearts or
        14 ounces canned
2   tablespoons butter
¼   teaspoon white pepper
¼   teaspoon dried sage or
        ¾ teaspoon of chopped fresh sage
1   tablespoon fresh Italian parsley, chopped,
        plus 4 sprigs for garnish

SERVES 4

Season the fillets with salt and pepper. Dust lightly with the soy flour. In a large skillet, heat 4 tablespoons of olive oil over moderately high heat and add the fillets. Gently brown the fillets on both sides. Transfer to a warmed platter; keep warm while you make the artichoke sauce.

In the same skillet, deglaze with the wine, scraping up any bits; add artichoke hearts, butter, white pepper, sage, and salt as needed. Reduce slightly and add parsley. Pour sauce over the fish and serve garnished with the parsley sprigs.

PER SERVING

Calories 329	Protein 26.5 grams	Carbohydrate 5.4 grams
Fiber 2.6 grams	Fat 20.5 grams	Net Carbs 2.8 grams

Roasted Trout with Herbs and Fennel

I was not a trout lover until I tasted this dish in a Florence restaurant last year. I immediately took out my pad and broke down the recipe. It's tough work but somebody has to do it! (Fresh herbs are the only way to go here.)

4	small trout, boned with head left on
1	small fennel bulb, halved and thinly sliced
4	sprigs fresh sage
4	sprigs fresh rosemary
4	sprigs fresh thyme
1	lemon, sliced into thin wedges
	Freshly ground black pepper
8	thin slices pancetta
	Olive oil

SERVES 4

Preheat the oven to 400°F. Lay the trout on a working surface with the cavity open. Divide and layer the fennel, herbs, and lemon in the cavity; sprinkle with pepper; then fold the fish closed. Using 1 slice of pancetta, gently wrap each fish in a diagonal motion, starting at the tail and finishing at the head. Use a second slice to wrap the fish from head to tail, forming a crisscross of pancetta around each fish.

Put the fish on an oiled roasting pan and roast for 10 minutes on each side until the pancetta is a dark golden color and the trout is firm to the touch.

PER SERVING

Calories 280	Protein 36.4 grams	Carbohydrate 3.2 grams
Fiber 1.4 grams	Fat 12.6 grams	Net Carbs 1.8 grams

Scallops Marinara

Scallops offer a truly different taste if naked and pampered in an olive oil bath, perfumed by garlic and onion. Do not overcook.

1   pound bay scallops or sea scallops,
      cut into quarters
1   small yellow onion, chopped
1   clove garlic, crushed
2   tablespoons olive oil
¼   teaspoon dried sage or
      ¾ teaspoon chopped fresh sage
½   cup white wine
4   fresh ripe plum tomatoes, chopped
1   teaspoon lemon juice
½   teaspoon white pepper
1   tablespoon chopped fresh Italian parsley
      Salt to taste *(optional)*

SERVES 4

In a medium skillet, sauté the onion and garlic in the olive oil until soft. Add the scallops and sauté lightly until opaque; do not overcook. Remove the scallops and keep warm.

Add the sage, wine, tomatoes, lemon juice, pepper, parsley, and salt to the skillet. Boil over high heat for 3 to 5 minutes until reduced slightly.

Return the scallops to the skillet, remove from the heat to marry with the sauce. Serve immediately.

PER SERVING

| Calories 163 | Protein 10.2 grams | Carbohydrate 6.6 grams |
| Fiber 1.2 grams | Fat 8.8 grams | Net Carbs 5.4 grams |

Mussels with Tomato Sauce

In Belgium, mussels are served with dignity and frites with mustard sauce.
The Italian version is served with love, wine, and tomato sauce. Enough said.

¼ cup extra virgin olive oil
½ medium yellow onion, thinly sliced
2 cloves garlic, sliced
48 mussels, scrubbed and debearded
¼ cup white wine
1 bay leaf
2 teaspoons chopped fresh Italian Parsley,
     plus sprigs for garnish
1 cup Tomato Sauce *(page 80)*
    Salt to taste
    Freshly ground black pepper to taste
1 tablespoon butter

SERVES 4

In a large skillet, heat the olive oil over moderately high heat. Sauté the onion until translucent; add the garlic and mussels and sauté until the mussels start to open, about 5 minutes. Add the wine, bay leaf, and chopped parsley; cover and cook for 3 to 5 minutes or until mussels have opened. Add the Tomato Sauce, salt, and pepper. Bring to a simmer, cook for 3 minutes, then stir in the butter. Arrange the mussels in a shallow bowl, discarding any unopened shells, and garnish with parsley sprigs.

PER SERVING

Calories 370   Protein 23.7 grams   Carbohydrate 11.9 grams
Fiber .99 grams   Fat 24 grams   NetCarbs 10.9 grams

Anchovy Peppers

As an anchovy lover, I've eaten fresh anchovies in Spain, Italy, Denmark, Sweden, and Holland. But still, this dish doesn't need anything special, it works well made with the canned variety available in all U.S. supermarkets.

2   medium red bell peppers
¼   cup extra virgin olive oil
     Salt to taste
     Freshly ground black pepper to taste
4   anchovies
2   tablespoons chopped fresh Italian parsley
8   basil leaves
¼   cup pitted calamata olives

SERVES 4

Preheat the oven to 350°F. Slice the bell peppers lengthwise into 4 pieces, discarding the stems, cores, and seeds. Arrange the peppers on a baking sheet, skin-side down, and drizzle with olive oil; then sprinkle with salt and pepper. Put half of an anchovy in the center of each piece of pepper, sprinkle with parsley, and bake 15 minutes or until the pepper begins to brown. When peppers are cool, arrange them on a platter. Garnish each piece with a basil leaf and sprinkle with olives.

PER SERVING

Calories 154	Protein 1.8 grams	Carbohydrate 4.5 grams
Fiber 1.6 grams	Fat 15 grams	Net Carbs 2.9 grams

CHAPTER SIX

Meat

CARNE

Meat Patties (POLPETTINI) with Rosemary Garlic Butter
Beef Medallions with Peppercorn Sauce
Beef Tenderloin Roasted in Herbs
Broiled Beef Flank Steak
Stuffed Beef (BRACIOLE)
Mixed Boiled (the famous BOLLITO MISTO) Dinner
Raisin Stuffed Meatballs in Tomato Sauce
Pork with Fennel
Pork with Olives
Grilled Pork Skewers with Radicchio
Pork Cutlets with Onions and Prosciutto
Deviled Pork Chops
Roast Pork
Sausages with Spinach and Onions
Sausages with Bell Peppers, Onions, and Fennel
Calf Liver with Sage Butter Sauce
Balsamic Liver and Onions

Veal Valdestana
Veal Chops Sorrentino
Veal Cutlet with Asparagus in Basil Sauce
Veal Loin Roast with Herbs
Veal Rolls with Cheese and Anchovy
Grilled Balsamic Veal Chops
Veal Fricassee with Sage and Lemon
Grilled Lamb Shoulder Chops
Oven Braised Lamb Shanks

Meat Patties with Rosemary Garlic Butter

POLPETTINI

Every culture has their meat patties—the Italians love their polpettini.
*Double the recipe and freeze the extras either cooked or raw, because they
make a great snack or lunch dish. To reheat them cooked, use the microwave.
They can be sliced and served with tomato sauce and cheese.*

½ pound ground pork
½ pound ground veal
½ pound lean ground beef
4 ounces sliced ham, minced
½ cup grated Parmesan cheese
4 egg yolks
1 tablespoon chopped fresh Italian parsley
2 cloves garlic, minced
2 teaspoons ground pepper
1 teaspoon salt
1 stick butter
3 tablespoons finely chopped fresh rosemary
    or 3 teaspoons dried rosemary
½ cup olive oil

SERVES 4

In a large mixing bowl, combine the pork, veal, and beef and mix well.
Add the ham, Parmesan, egg yolks, parsley, garlic, pepper, and salt.
Mix thoroughly, cover, and chill.

In a small bowl, mash the garlic and butter and rosemary
together until well blended. Season the butter with salt and pepper
and chill. Divide the meat mixture into 8 equal portions. Shape
each portion into a ball, insert 1 tablespoon of the rosemary garlic
butter into the center, and flatten into a patty, sealing in the butter.
Chill the patties.

Preheat the oven to 400°F. Heat the olive oil in a large non-stick ovenproof skillet over moderately high heat. Sear each patty until golden, 3 to 5 minutes. Turn and sear on the other side. Put the skillet into the oven for 8 to 10 minutes or until no longer pink inside. Let the patties rest 3 minutes before serving.

PER SERVING

Calories 872	Protein 42 grams	Carbohydrate 2.3 grams
Fiber .56 grams	Fat 77.6 grams	Net Carbs 1.7 grams

Beef Medallions with Peppercorn Sauce

I don't remember exactly when I developed this Peppercorn Sauce, but I remember every time I serve it my guests go crazy and everyone wants the recipe. Of course, you can serve this sauce with other cuts of meat. Be creative.

24	ounces beef filet, cut into 4 medallions
	Salt to taste
	White pepper to taste
¼	cup olive oil
2	tablespoons butter
½	medium yellow onion, minced
1	medium shallot, minced
1	tablespoon green peppercorns, in brine
1	clove garlic, minced
½	teaspoon dried thyme or
	1½ teaspoons chopped fresh thyme
1	bay leaf
½	cup white wine
1	cup Chicken Stock *(page 61)*
1	cup heavy cream

SERVES 4

Season the meat with salt and pepper and set aside. Heat the olive oil in a large nonstick skillet over moderately high heat, and sear the medallions on both sides. After the medallions are browned, continue to cook over moderate heat until done to preference. Transfer the medallions to a warmed serving platter and keep warm while you prepare the sauce.

To the same skillet, add the butter and sauté the onion and shallot until soft. Add the peppercorns, garlic, thyme, and bay leaf, and sauté for 1 minute. Deglaze the skillet with white wine; add stock, scraping up any brown bits and reducing slightly. Add the cream, season with salt and pepper, and simmer for 5 minutes, or until slightly thickened. Pour the sauce over the beef medallions, remove bay leaf, and serve immediately.

PER SERVING

Calories 409	Protein 1.8 grams	Carbohydrate 4.5 grams
Fiber .55 grams	Fat 41.5 grams	Net Carbs 3.9 grams

Beef Tenderloin Roasted in Herbs

The simplicity of Italian cooking is demonstrated here—when fresh beef and fresh herbs hit the hot oil. Use fresh herbs, if at all possible, and make sure the oven reaches the 400°F mark. This dish has a superb taste.

4   8-ounce pieces beef tenderloin
2   teaspoons finely chopped fresh rosemary or
     ¾ teaspoon dried rosemary
2   teaspoons finely chopped fresh thyme or
     ¾ teaspoon dried thyme
2   teaspoons finely chopped fresh parsley or
     ¾ teaspoon dried parsley
2   teaspoons finely chopped fresh oregano or
     1 teaspoon dried
     Salt to taste
     Freshly ground black pepper
¼   cup olive oil

SERVES 4

Preheat the oven to 400°F.

Season each piece of tenderloin with salt and pepper. Using a piece of trussing string, tie each tenderloin on the side to make a round shape. Combine the herbs in a shallow bowl. Press the pieces of beef into the herbs, coating them completely. Set aside.

Heat the olive oil in a heavy ovenproof skillet over moderately high heat. Carefully add the meat, taking care not to crowd the skillet. Sear the meat on both sides until the herbs start to brown and the meat caramelizes. Put the skillet in the oven for 5 minutes for medium rare.

PER SERVING

Calories 741	Protein 41 grams	Carbohydrate .37 grams
Fiber .08 grams	Fat 62.8 grams	Net Carbs .3 grams

Broiled Beef Flank Steak

If you can't get flank steak, don't worry, this works equally well with skirt steak.
Don't omit the anchovies, because they are needed in this taste duo.

2   pounds beef flank steak
½   cup extra virgin olive oil, plus 1 tablespoon
2   stalks celery, finely chopped
3   fresh plum tomatoes, minced
½   cup pitted, chopped calamata olives
½   cup pitted, chopped green olives
¼   cup capers
3   tablespoons chopped fresh Italian parsley
2   anchovies, minced
3   cloves garlic, minced
½   teaspoon red pepper flakes
    Salt to taste
    Freshly ground black pepper to taste
¼   cup water *(optional)*

SERVES 4

Preheat the broiler. In a small mixing bowl, combine ½ cup of olive oil, celery, tomatoes, olives, capers, parsley, anchovies, half the garlic, and the red pepper flakes. Adjust the seasoning with salt and pepper. If the mixture is dry, add up to ¼ cup water. Mix well and set this veggie sauce aside.

Rub the flank steak with the tablespoon of olive oil, the remaining garlic, and salt and pepper. Broil the steak 10 minutes or until well browned, then turn and broil another 8 to 10 minutes or until nearly done to taste. Let the meat rest 5 minutes, then slice into pieces ¼-inch thick. Spoon the sauce over slices and serve.

PER SERVING

Calories 661	Protein 49 grams	Carbohydrate 6 grams
Fiber 2.2 grams	Fat 48.8 grams	Net Carbs 3.8 grams

Stuffed Beef

BRACIOLE

Stuffed round steak, braciole is a mainstay in "Sunday's Gravy."
Ours was influenced by my Dad's love of raisins (Sicilian style), which
created Mom's version. Normally, there would be double the amount
of raisins, but in order to keep the carbs low, I reduced them. Forgive
me, Pop. Mom, I did remember to plump the raisins in wine.

3 tablespoons olive oil, divided
1 small yellow onion, minced
2 cloves garlic, minced
2 tablespoons grated Romano cheese
2 tablespoons chopped fresh Italian parsley
1½ tablespoons white raisins, plumped in wine
¼ cup pine nuts, toasted *(see page 28)*
   Freshly ground black pepper to taste
   Salt to taste *(optional)*
2 pounds beef top round steak,
   about ¼ inch thick, then pounded thin
3 cups marinara sauce

SERVES 6

Pound the beef.

In a medium bowl, mix 2 tablespoons of the olive oil with the rest of the ingredients except the beef and marinara sauce.

Spread this filling over the steak. Roll up, jelly roll fashion; then tie securely in several places with string. Can be cut into smaller pieces for easier handling.

Heat the remaining tablespoon of olive oil in a skillet and brown the braciole. Drain off any remaining oil and add the sauce. Simmer, covered, for 1½ to 2 hours, or until the meat is very tender. Remove the string before serving.

PER SERVING

Calories 430	Protein 36.8 grams	Carbohydrate 14.6 grams
Fiber 2.6 grams	Fat 24 grams	Net Carbs 12 grams

Mixed Boiled Dinner

THE FAMOUS *BOLLITO MISTO*

Bollito misto *means "mixed boiled" and it is traditionally served at large gatherings, usually for a special holiday meal, although that seems to be changing these days, as this meal is now served more frequently. This version was developed as an everyday meal and feeds four.*

1	gallon water
1	medium carrot, chopped
1	large onion, halved and cut into ½-inch slices
1	small celery root, cut into ½-inch pieces
4	sprigs fresh Italian parsley
1	clove garlic
1	bay leaf
	Salt to taste
1	teaspoon black peppercorns
2	chicken legs with thighs, cut into 4 pieces
1	pound beef brisket
4	Italian sausages
1	cup Green Sauce *(page 78)*

SERVES 4

In a large soup pot, combine the water, carrot, onion, celery root, parsley, garlic, bay leaf, salt, and peppercorns. Bring to a boil; reduce heat to low and simmer for 30 minutes. Add the chicken and beef, and continue to simmer without boiling for about 60 minutes. Add the sausages and continue to cook for 30 minutes. Transfer the beef to a cutting board and slice. Arrange the beef, chicken, and sausages on a large warm serving platter; drizzle with cooking liquid and large dollops of Green Sauce.

PER SERVING

Calories 980	Protein 53.5 grams	Carbohydrate 3.2 grams
Fiber .63 grams	Fat 82.8 grams	Net Carbs 2.6 grams

Raisin Stuffed Meatballs in Tomato Sauce

Pop loved raisins in his meatballs. Mom did not, so the ones with the toothpicks were for Dad. Oh, what great Sunday dinners we had with these great meatballs! I was with Mom, I didn't like the raisins, and yes, they can be omitted (less carbs).

1	pound ground beef
½	pound ground pork
½	cup chopped red onion
½	cup grated Parmesan cheese
1	egg
2	tablespoons chopped fresh Italian parsley
2	tablespoons pine nuts, toasted *(see page 28)*
2	teaspoons chopped fresh thyme or
	1 teaspoon dried thyme
1	teaspoon minced garlic
	Salt to taste
	Freshly ground black pepper to taste
¼	cup raisins
¼–⅓	cup olive oil
2	cups Tomato Sauce *(page 80)*

YIELDS 28 PIECES

In a medium-sized bowl, combine the beef, pork, onion, Parmesan, egg, parsley, pine nuts, thyme, garlic, salt, and pepper until well mixed. Form the mixture into 1½-inch balls. Make a hole in the center of each meatball with your finger, insert 2 raisins into the center, then press the hole closed.

Heat ¼ cup of olive oil in a large skillet over moderately high heat. Gradually add the meatballs without overcrowding the pan, and brown well on all sides, adding more oil if necessary. Stir in the Tomato Sauce, reduce the heat to moderately low, cover, and simmer 25 to 30 minutes or until meat is no longer pink inside and flavors have blended. Serve with Parmesan cheese on the side.

PER MEATBALL

Calories 94	Protein 5.8 grams	Carbohydrate 2 grams
Fiber .26 grams	Fat 7 grams	Net Carbs 1.7 grams

Pork with Fennel

*Fennel (anise), often called Italian celery, is a great complement to pork,
as evidenced by the addition of fennel seeds to Italian sausages.
If you've never cooked with fennel before, you're in for a great treat.*

3   tablespoons olive oil, divided
4   large, thick pork chops
     Salt to taste
     Freshly ground black pepper
½   cup white wine
1   medium fennel bulb, quartered
        and cut into ¼-inch slices
4   garlic cloves, minced
2   fresh ripe plum tomatoes, chopped
1   tablespoon chopped fresh tarragon or
        1 teaspoon dried tarragon
½   cup Chicken Stock *(page 61)*

SERVES 4

In a skillet large enough to hold all the ingredients, heat the 2 tablespoons olive oil over moderately high heat. Season the pork chops with salt and pepper, add to the skillet, and brown on both sides. Transfer the pork to a plate; add wine to the skillet and reduce by half, scraping any brown bits from the bottom of the skillet. Transfer the liquid to a small bowl and reserve.

Wash and dry the skillet. Add the remaining tablespoon of olive oil to the skillet and sauté the fennel and garlic for 5 minutes. Add tomatoes, tarragon, Chicken Stock, reserved wine reduction, and salt and pepper to taste. Return the pork chops to the pan, piling the fennel on top; cover and simmer for 40 minutes or until the pork is tender.

PER SERVING

Calories 489	Protein 52.7 grams	Carbohydrate 7 grams
Fiber 2.2 grams	Fat 24.8 grams	Net Carbs 4.8 grams

Pork with Olives

Olives take center stage in this recipe, and the quality of the olives is paramount to a great-tasting dish. This means that you will have to use calamata olives, period. You'll thank me for warning you.

¾ cup white wine
¼ cup olive oil
1 tablespoon white wine vinegar
2 bay leaves
1 teaspoon dried thyme or
   1 tablespoon chopped fresh thyme
1 clove garlic
   Salt to taste
   Freshly ground black pepper
1½ pounds boneless pork loin
1 tablespoon butter
1 cup pitted calamata olives

SERVES 4

In a small bowl, whisk together wine, olive oil, vinegar, bay leaves, thyme, garlic, salt, and pepper. Put the pork in a glass or stainless bowl and pour the marinade over, turning to coat well. Marinate the pork 2 hours in the refrigerator.

Remove the pork from the marinade, reserving the marinade. Pat the pork dry with paper towels. Heat the butter in a heavy, deep pot with a lid. Brown the pork on all sides, add the marinade and olives, cover, and simmer over low heat for 30 minutes or until pork is tender. Discard bay leaves. Serve with the pan juices.

PER SERVING

Calories 537	Protein 35.6 grams	Carbohydrate 6 grams
Fiber 1.2 grams	Fat 37.6 grams	Net Carbs 4.8 grams

Grilled Pork Skewers with Radicchio

I've done a million grilling segments on TV, and this is the universal favorite. Actually, it's one of my personal favorites, too. (If you are using wooden skewers, remember to soak them first.)

1½ pounds boneless pork loin
2   small heads radicchio, round variety
2   small red onions
⅓   cup extra virgin olive oil
1   tablespoon chopped fresh rosemary or
      1 teaspoon dried rosemary
3   cloves garlic, minced
    Salt to taste
    Freshly ground black pepper to taste
    Lemon wedges

SERVES 4

Cut the pork into 1½-inch cubes and set aside. Trim ¼ inch from the bottom of the radicchio. Leaving the core intact, cut each head of radicchio into 8 wedges. Peel and cut each onion lengthwise into 8 wedges, leaving the root end intact. Assemble 8 skewers by alternating 4 to 6 pieces of the meat, 2 of radicchio, and 2 of onion on each skewer. Lay the skewers on a baking dish. Combine the olive oil, rosemary, garlic, salt, and pepper in a small bowl. Rub some of this mixture on each skewer, cover, and marinate in the refrigerator for at least 1 hour.

Preheat the grill. Remove skewers from the marinade, shaking off any excess. Grill the skewers on a lightly oiled grill until pork and vegetables are golden and tender and the pork is cooked through, about 10 to 12 minutes total. Serve with lemon wedges.

PER SERVING

Calories 496	Protein 36.5 grams	Carbohydrate 6.2 grams
Fiber 1.2 grams	Fat 35.6 grams	Net Carbs 5 grams

Pork Cutlets with Onions and Prosciutto

*I'm a big fan of boneless pork cutlets. They are so versatile and provide
a great alternative to chicken or veal. They also have a great flavor
and are not easily overpowered by cooking sauces. Pork and tomato sauce
is one of life's great-tasting combinations—a "perfect relationship."*

½   cup olive oil
8   small boneless pork cutlets,
       about 4–6 ounces each, ¾ inch thick
    Salt to taste
    Freshly ground black pepper to taste
2   tablespoons butter
2   medium yellow onions, thinly sliced
4   slices prosciutto, chopped
2   cloves garlic, minced
½   cup white wine
½   cup Tomato Sauce *(page 80)*
1   tablespoon chopped fresh Italian parsley

SERVES 4

Heat the oil in a large nonstick skillet over moderately high heat.
Season the cutlets with salt and pepper and brown them on both sides;
then lower heat and finish cooking until no traces of pink remain,
about 10 minutes more. As the cutlets are finished, transfer them to a
warmed serving platter and keep warm.

To the same skillet, add the butter and onions and sauté on medium heat until the onions are soft, 5 to 8 minutes. Add the prosciutto
and garlic and sauté until golden, 3 to 5 minutes. Increase the heat
and deglaze the skillet with the wine, reducing slightly. Add the
Tomato Sauce and simmer for 8 minutes. Return the cutlets to the
skillet and coat with the sauce. Sprinkle with parsley and serve.

PER SERVING

Calories 775	Protein 50.8 grams	Carbohydrate 7 grams
Fiber 1.4 grams	Fat 57.9 grams	Net Carbs 5.6 grams

Deviled Pork Chops

I love crushed red peppers and was in heaven when I had them in Castelmolas, Sicily, in a very local restaurant. This recipe should emphasize that cooking can be easy and great eating does not necessitate spending hours in the kitchen.

4	large pork chops, 2 inches thick
¼	cup olive oil
	Salt to taste
	Freshly ground black pepper
1	tablespoon red pepper flakes
1	teaspoon dried rosemary or
	1 tablespoon chopped fresh rosemary
1	lemon cut in wedges

SERVES 4

Preheat the oven to 450°F. Arrange the chops on a shallow dish. In a small mixing bowl, whisk the olive oil, salt, pepper, pepper flakes, and rosemary. Rub the mixture on all surfaces of the pork. Refrigerate for at least 30 minutes.

Heat the olive oil in an ovenproof skillet over moderately high heat and sear the pork chops on one side. Turn the pork over and transfer immediately to the oven. Cook until there is no pink in the center. Garnish with lemon wedges and serve.

PER SERVING

Calories 320	Protein 26.2 grams	Carbohydrate 1.1 grams
Fiber .60 grams	Fat 23 grams	Net Carbs .5 grams

Roast Pork

Recently it was suggested to a family member whose baby was suffering from acid reflux to give her cool fennel-seed tea, which you make by boiling water with fennel seeds and letting it cool. Well, here the fennel seeds (available in your supermarket) are used in the most traditional Italian way, to permeate the pork as it slow roasts. Maybe that's why my tummy feels so good after eating this dish.

4½–5 pounds boneless pork loin
1   tablespoon dried rosemary or
       3 tablespoons chopped fresh rosemary
4   cloves garlic, minced
1   teaspoon fennel seeds
2   tablespoons olive oil
1   tablespoon fresh lemon juice
    Freshly ground black pepper to taste
    Salt to taste *(optional)*

SERVES 6

Preheat the oven to 425°F. In a small bowl, mix the rosemary, garlic, fennel seeds, olive oil, lemon juice, pepper, and salt. Spread over the top and sides of the pork as far as it will go.

Place the pork in a roasting pan and tent with aluminum foil. Roast for 20 minutes; then reduce the oven temperature to 375°F and bake for an additional 1½ to 2 hours or until the internal meat temperature is 180°F. Remove foil for the last hour of oventime

Remove from the oven and let rest for 20 minutes before carving.

PER SERVING

Calories 611	Protein 77 grams	Carbohydrate 1.7 grams
Fiber .64 grams	Fat 30.6 grams	Net Carbs 1.1 grams

Sausages with Spinach and Onions

This is a very traditional Italian dish. Sausages are often cooked with some type of green leafy vegetable. In this recipe, I prefer spinach (which was introduced into Europe by the Moors around A.D. 1000).

5	tablespoons olive oil, divided
8	Italian-style sausages, hot or sweet
2	medium yellow onions, thinly sliced
2	cloves garlic, chopped
	Salt to taste
	Freshly ground black pepper to taste
1½	pounds spinach, washed and stems trimmed
1	cup Tomato Sauce *(page 80)*
½	cup scallions, thinly sliced
2	tablespoons chopped fresh Italian parsley

SERVES 4

Preheat the oven to 350°F. Coat a large baking dish with 1 tablespoon of the olive oil and arrange the sausages on the dish. Cook the sausages in the oven for 30 minutes or until nicely browned and no longer pink inside. Meanwhile prepare the spinach.

Heat the remaining olive oil in a skillet over moderate heat. Add the yellow onions and garlic and season with salt and pepper. Sauté the onions until limp, then cover loosely with foil. Continue to cook, stirring occasionally, until the onions are golden and caramelized, about 15 minutes. Increase the heat to moderately high and add the spinach, sautéing until the spinach is wilted. Stir in the Tomato Sauce, and simmer for 5 minutes.

When the sausages are done, spread the spinach mixture on a warmed serving platter and arrange the sausages on top. Sprinkle with the green onions and parsley and serve.

PER SERVING

Calories 793	Protein 39.7 grams	Carbohydrate 17.6 grams
Fiber 6.7 grams	Fat 63 grams	Net Carbs 10.9 grams

Sausages with Bell Peppers, Onions, and Fennel

In Manhattan and the surrounding boroughs of New York City, we are fortunate to have real Italian pork stores. Trust me, real Italian sausages are superior to the supermarket variety. So take a plane, a train, and get some real Italian sausages.

4	tablespoons olive oil, divided
6	sweet or hot Italian sausages, halved
1	medium yellow onion, cut into ½-inch strips
1	medium red bell pepper, cut into ½-inch strips
1	medium green bell pepper, cut into ½-inch strips
1	small fennel bulb, cored and cut into strips
3	cloves garlic, chopped
2	cups red wine, divided
2	fresh plum tomatoes, seeded and chopped
2	teaspoons chopped fresh oregano
	or ¾ teaspoon dried oregano
½	teaspoon fennel seeds
	Salt to taste
	Freshly ground black pepper
	Grated Parmesan cheese

SERVES 4

Heat 2 tablespoons of the olive oil in a large skillet with a lid over moderately high heat. Pierce the sausages in several places with the tines of a fork, and add to the skillet.

Brown the sausages on all sides, turning frequently, then transfer the sausages to a plate. Set aside.

In the same skillet, heat the remaining olive oil over moderate heat and add the onion, red and green bell peppers, fennel, and garlic; sauté until onion begins to soften, 5 to 8 minutes. Add ½ cup of wine and return the sausages to the skillet; use the remaining wine to deglaze the pan, scraping up any brown bits from the bottom of the skillet. Add the tomatoes, oregano, fennel seeds, salt, and pepper. Bring the mixture to a boil, then reduce heat to low, cover, and simmer. Cook for 30 minutes or until the sausages are no longer pink inside and the flavors have blended.

Transfer the sausages to a warmed serving platter. Pile the vegetables on top and pour the sauce over all. Serve with Parmesan cheese.

PER SERVING

Calories 658	Protein 27 grams	Carbohydrate 15.7 grams
Fiber 3.5 grams	Fat 46 grams	Net Carbs 12.2 grams

Calf Liver with Sage Butter Sauce

Calves liver is sweeter, more delicate than the older beef version Mom would fix for dinner; it always seemed to turn green. Although she smothered it with onions my brother and I would survive dinner on mashed potatoes.

1½–2 cups milk
    (carb count is not included in milk bath)
1¼ pounds calf liver, sliced thin
    Soy flour for dusting
2 eggs, beaten
    Freshly ground black pepper
    Salt
1 tablespoon extra virgin olive oil
½ cup butter
1 teaspoon dried sage or
    1 tablespoon chopped fresh sage
1 large shallot, minced

SERVES 4

Soak the liver in the milk for a few minutes, then dust each piece with soy flour; dip in egg and season with pepper and salt.

In a large skillet, sauté the liver briskly in the hot olive oil and butter. When cooked to your liking, remove liver to hot platter. Add sage and shallot to skillet and simmer for a minute or two, check salt, and pour over liver. Serve immediately.

PER SERVING

Calories 465	Protein 28.8 grams	Carbohydrate 7.5 grams
Fiber .10 grams	Fat 35.3 grams	Net Carbs 7.4 grams

Balsamic Liver and Onions

Although I'm not generally a fan of beef liver, it works nicely in this recipe. The balsamic vinegar reduces to a sweet sauce that tempers the taste of the beef liver.

3   tablespoons butter
3   tablespoons olive oil
¼   pound pancetta, chopped
2   medium yellow onions, thinly sliced
     Salt to taste
     Freshly ground black pepper to taste
1½ pounds beef liver, cut into ½-inch strips
2   tablespoons balsamic vinegar
¼   cup chopped fresh Italian parsley

SERVES 4

In a large skillet, heat the butter and olive oil over moderate heat. Sauté the pancetta 2 to 3 minutes or until translucent but not browned. Add the onions, salt, and pepper and sauté until the onions are golden brown, about 10 minutes. Add the liver, stir well to combine, and cook for 5 to 6 minutes until there is no trace of pink inside; then add the vinegar. Increase the heat to moderately high and cook until the sauce has reduced a bit and thickened. Stir in the parsley and serve.

PER SERVING

Calories 425	Protein 31.5 grams	Carbohydrate 8.9 grams
Fiber 1.1 grams	Fat 29 grams	Net Carbs 7.8 grams

Veal Valdestana

Back to the Coney Island, New York, of my youth and to Papa "Gino," who made my favorite Valdestana. Here, I have substituted soy flour for a marvelous interpretation. The original recipe comes from Valle d'Aosta, northern Italy, which is near the Swiss border. Hence the cream cheese, which replaces the fontina cheese from this valley.

8   veal cutlets
4   tablespoons cream cheese
1   tablespoon fresh Italian parsley, chopped
¼   teaspoon dried sage or
      ¾ teaspoon chopped fresh sage
4   slices prosciutto
4   large white mushrooms, sliced
1   cup soy flour
3   tablespoons unsalted butter
3   tablespoons extra virgin olive oil
½   cup white wine
      Salt and freshly ground black pepper to taste

SERVES 4

Pound veal; mix cream cheese, parsley, and sage. Spread the mixture over 4 veal slices, add slice of prosciutto and divide mushrooms over each. Top with veal slice and seal edges of sandwich by pounding all around edges. Dip in soy flour.

Sauté on both sides in the butter and olive oil until golden, then reduce to a simmer. Add wine, salt, pepper. Cover, cook about 6 to 8 minutes, and serve.

PER SERVING

| Calories 806 | Protein 60.3 grams | Carbohydrate 8.4 grams |
| Fiber 2.3 grams | Fat 56.8 grams | Net Carbs 6.1 grams |

Veal Chops Sorrentino

*Here is a dish (probably originated in Sorrento) that can be your romantic
meal or conquest dinner. Light the candles; use cloth napkins; play some
great music, Italian of course; and serve with a bottle of Merlot (Bolla,
my favorite). Oh, did I mention to put the kids to bed first?*

4	large veal chops, bone in
4	tablespoons olive oil, divided
	Salt to taste
	Freshly ground black pepper to taste
1	tablespoon butter
1	clove garlic, minced
3	fresh plum tomatoes, peeled, seeded, and finely chopped
¼	cup chopped ham
1	teaspoon chopped fresh oregano or ⅓ teaspoon dried oregano
2	tablespoons chopped fresh Italian parsley
1	cup shredded mozzarella
½	cup grated Parmesan cheese

SERVES 4

Rub the chops with 2 tablespoons of the olive oil, then season with salt and pepper. Set aside while you start the sauce.

Melt the butter in a medium skillet over moderate heat. Add the garlic and sauté until golden, 1 to 2 minutes. Add tomatoes and ham and cook until the tomatoes start to break down. Stir in the oregano and parsley and cook for 5 minutes. Remove the skillet from the heat and stir in the mozzarella. Set the mixture aside while you prepare the veal.

Preheat the broiler. In a large skillet, heat the remaining 2 tablespoons of olive oil over moderately high heat. Cook the veal chops 6 to 8 minutes on each side until golden brown and done to taste. Remove the veal chops from the skillet and arrange on a broiler pan. Top each chop with a quarter of the tomato mixture, sprinkle with Parmesan, and broil until the top is bubbly. Serve immediately.

PER SERVING

Calories 524	Protein 45 grams	Carbohydrate 3.6 grams
Fiber .59 grams	Fat 36 grams	Net Carbs 3 grams

Veal Cutlet with Asparagus in Basil Sauce

On one trip to Sicily, I stopped in Forza d'Agro' to see this very old Sicilian village and checked out the location where Al Pacino's character in The Godfather *got married. Since it was too early for lunch, we decided to drive on to Messina, where we'd enjoy a big dinner. Once there, I found a little restaurant where I ate this delicious veal in basil sauce and washed it down with lots of wine because I didn't have to drive. Now you don't have to go to Sicily to enjoy this dish.*

1	pound asparagus
1½	pounds veal scallopine
	Soy flour for dusting
3	tablespoons butter
3	tablespoons olive oil
¼	cup minced shallots
½	pound white mushrooms, thinly sliced
½	cup white wine
⅓	cup Pesto Sauce *(page 77)*
½	cup heavy cream
	Salt and pepper to taste

SERVES 4

Bring a large saucepan of salted water to a boil and prepare an ice-water bath. Trim the tough ends from the asparagus and cut the spears, on the bias, into 2- to 3-inch lengths. When the water is boiling, add the asparagus and blanch until al dente. With a wire basket or slotted spoon, scoop the asparagus from the water and submerge in the ice-water bath. When the asparagus has cooled, drain and pat dry on paper towels. Set aside.

Dust the veal with the soy flour, shaking off excess. In a large skillet, heat the butter and olive oil over moderately high heat. When the foam subsides and the fats are hot, slip the veal into the pan and brown on one side, turn, and continue to cook until tender. Transfer the veal to a plate as it browns and keep warm.

Add the shallots and mushrooms to the skillet and sauté over moderate heat, stirring frequently, until the mushrooms are tender and shallots are golden. Deglaze the skillet with wine, scraping up any brown bits, and reduce the wine slightly. In a small bowl, combine the Pesto Sauce and cream, then add this mixture to the skillet. Heat slightly, adjust the seasoning with salt and pepper, and return the veal and asparagus with any juices to the skillet. Heat through and serve immediately.

PER SERVING

Calories 807	Protein 45.8 grams	Carbohydrate 8.2 grams
Fiber 2 grams	Fat 64 grams	Net Carbs 6.2 grams

Veal Loin Roast with Herbs

It was the olive harvest in the Molise region during my annual pilgrimage. After participating in olive picking and watching them being pressed into olive oil, we had worked up an appetite, so our hosts prepared a luncheon feast that was not to be believed. I bet there was every item this region produces on the several buffet tables, and this simple veal roast, my favorite. When you prepare it, use fresh herbs—it makes a difference.

2	pounds veal loin roast, tied
	Salt to taste
	Freshly ground black pepper to taste
1	teaspoon chopped fresh sage or
	⅓ teaspoon dried sage
1	teaspoon chopped fresh rosemary or
	⅓ teaspoon dried rosemary
1	teaspoon chopped fresh thyme or
	⅓ teaspoon dried thyme
3	cloves garlic, minced
¼	cup olive oil, divided
2	tablespoons butter

SERVES 4

Preheat the oven to 425°F. Season the veal with salt and pepper. Combine the sage, rosemary, thyme, and garlic in a small bowl and mash with a fork to blend together. Slowly incorporate 2 tablespoons of the olive oil, making a paste. Rub the paste over the entire surface of the veal.

Put the butter and the remaining olive oil in a roasting pan; add the veal and roast for 15 minutes. Reduce the heat to 375°F and roast until the internal temperature is 145°, about 30 to 40 minutes. Let the veal stand for 10 minutes before slicing into ¼-inch slices.

PER SERVING

Calories 456	Protein 42.6 grams	Carbohydrate .86 grams
Fiber .10 grams	Fat 30.5 grams	Net Carbs .76 grams

Veal Rolls with Cheese and Anchovy

Anchovies are so nutritious, and the combination of the cheese paired with veal is a five-star recipe. Remember, before using canned or jarred anchovies, rinse in cool water to remove excess salt. Enjoy!

1	pound veal cutlets
4	ounces shredded mozzarella
½	cup grated Parmesan
8–10	anchovy fillets
	Salt to taste
	Freshly ground black pepper to taste
¼	cup olive oil
½	cup white wine
2	cups beef stock
2	tablespoons chopped fresh Italian parsley, divided
2	tablespoons butter

SERVES 4

Pound the cutlets between two pieces of plastic wrap with a meat mallet until thin, about ⅛ inch thick. Lay the cutlets out on a work surface and sprinkle some of the mozzarella and Parmesan on each. Put an anchovy on top and season with salt and pepper. Roll the cutlets up, starting at one long end. Secure with toothpicks or kitchen twine.

In a large skillet, heat the olive oil over moderately high heat. Brown the veal rolls on all sides without crowding the skillet. Deglaze the skillet with the wine, scraping up any brown bits. Add the stock and 1 tablespoon of parsley, cover, and reduce the heat to low. Simmer for about 20 minutes or until veal is tender. Transfer the rolls to a warmed platter. Remove the toothpicks or twine and keep warm.

Remove the pan from the heat before whisking in the butter and remaining parsley. Adjust the seasoning with salt and pepper and pour over the veal rolls.

PER SERVING

Calories 608	Protein 41.1 grams	Carbohydrate 3 grams
Fiber .31 grams	Fat 45 grams	Net Carbs 2.7 grams

Grilled Balsamic Veal Chops

Buy some big veal chops and prepare yourself to be amazed at how much you'll love the taste of this simple, straightforward recipe.

¼ cup chopped fresh thyme or
     1¼ tablespoons dried thyme
4 cloves garlic, chopped
3 tablespoons extra virgin olive oil
2 tablespoons balsamic vinegar
    Salt to taste
    Freshly ground black pepper
4 large veal chops
2 tablespoons chopped fresh Italian parsley

SERVES 4

In a small bowl, combine the thyme, garlic, olive oil, vinegar, salt, and pepper. Place the veal chops in a single layer on a plate and rub all surfaces with the thyme mixture. Cover and refrigerate for at least 1 hour. Meanwhile, heat the grill.

Grill the veal chops over moderate heat for 5 to 8 minutes on each side, or until the exterior is slightly charred and the center is pink. Sprinkle with parsley and serve.

PER SERVING

Calories 322	Protein 33 grams	Carbohydrate 2.9 grams
Fiber .46 grams	Fat 19 grams	Net Carbs 2.4 grams

Veal Fricassee with Sage and Lemon

The perfect dish for a weekend meal when there is time to cook.
There is nothing like the aroma of a cooking stew wafting through the
air to make a house a home. The smell of a great meal cooking—
can you think of anything that says, "I love you" any better?

2	ounces dried porcini mushrooms
½	cup warm water
3	tablespoons extra virgin olive oil, divided
3	tablespoons butter, divided
1	medium red onion, chopped
1	medium carrot, chopped
1	medium stalk celery, chopped
2	cloves garlic, chopped
2	tablespoons chopped fresh sage
	or 2 teaspoons dried sage
1½	pounds veal stew meat, cut into 1-inch cubes
	Salt to taste
	Freshly ground black pepper to taste
2	tablespoons soy flour for dusting
½	cup white wine
2	cups Chicken Stock *(page 61)*
2	egg yolks
2	teaspoons freshly squeezed lemon juice

SERVES 4

In a small bowl, combine the porcini and water and set aside.

Heat 1 tablespoon each of the olive oil and butter in a large, deep skillet over moderate heat. Sauté the onion, carrot, and celery until onion is translucent, about 5 minutes. Add the garlic and sage, reduce heat to low, and cook slowly until vegetables begin to color, about 8 to 10 minutes.

Season the veal with salt and pepper. Dust with soy flour and toss to coat. Heat the remaining olive oil and butter in a medium skillet and brown the veal in batches without crowding the skillet. As the meat browns, transfer the cubes to the skillet with vegetables. Deglaze the pan with wine, scraping up any brown bits and adding them to the veal along with the stock, the porcini and their soaking liquid, and salt and pepper to taste. Bring the mixture to a boil, cover, and reduce heat to low; simmer until veal is very tender, about 1 hour.

Whisk the egg yolks and lemon juice together in a small bowl; then gradually whisk ½ cup of the veal cooking liquid into the egg yolk mixture. Stir this mixture back into the veal and heat through before serving.

PER SERVING

Calories 515	Protein 47 grams	Carbohydrate 13.9 grams
Fiber 3.7 grams	Fat 27.6 grams	Net Carbs 10.2 grams

Grilled Lamb Shoulder Chops

*In this recipe I use lemons to enhance the flavor of the meat. Lemon juice
works just as well on meat as it does on fish, but it's surprising to me that
fact is not well known outside of the Mediterranean. The all-important
lemon zest in this marinade really infuses lemon flavor into the chops.*

8   lamb shoulder chops, about ¾ inch thick
     Salt to taste
     Freshly ground black pepper to taste
½   cup olive oil
     Zest of 2 lemons and juice of 1 lemon
2   tablespoons chopped fresh sage or
        2 teaspoons dried sage
3   cloves garlic, minced
2   tablespoons chopped fresh Italian parsley

SERVES 4

Season the lamb chops with salt and pepper. In a small bowl, combine
the olive oil, zest, sage, and garlic. Rub the mixture over the entire
surface of the lamb chops. Cover and marinate in the refrigerator for
at least 1 hour.

Preheat the grill. Remove the lamb from the marinade, shaking
off any excess. Lightly oil the grill and cook the lamb on one side
until bottom is well browned, about 2 minutes. Turn the chops over
and cook about 2 more minutes for medium-rare or 2½ minutes for
medium. Sprinkle with the lemon juice and parsley and serve.

PER SERVING

Calories 367	Protein 45.5 grams	Carbohydrate 1.5 grams
Fiber .20 grams	Fat 18.9 grams	Net Carbs 1.3 grams

Oven Braised Lamb Shanks

After walking and shopping Vucciria Market in Palermo, I fell into this neighborhood restaurant. The oven braised lamb shanks were so succulent that I pleaded with the chef to write out the recipe for me. He did, sort of. And here, after many delicious redo's, is my Braised Lamb Shanks.

3	tablespoons extra virgin olive oil, divided
3	tablespoons butter, divided
1	cup chopped yellow onion
½	cup chopped carrot
½	cup chopped celery
1	tablespoon chopped garlic
4	lamb shanks
	Salt to taste
	Freshly ground black pepper to taste
1	cup white wine
2	cups Chicken Stock (*page 61*)
3	fresh plum tomatoes, chopped
4	2-inch strips lemon zest
1	tablespoon chopped fresh rosemary
	or 1 teaspoon of dried rosemary
1	teaspoon chopped fresh thyme
	or ⅓ teaspoon of dried thyme
1	bay leaf
¼	cup chopped parsley

SERVES 4

Preheat the oven to 350°F.

In a large skillet, heat 1 tablespoon each of the olive oil and butter and sauté the onion, carrot, celery, and garlic until the onion is translucent. Transfer the vegetables to a Dutch oven and set aside.

Season the lamb shanks with salt and pepper. In the same skillet, heat the remaining olive oil and butter over moderately high heat. Brown 2 of the lamb shanks on all sides and transfer to the Dutch oven; repeat with the remaining lamb. Add the wine and deglaze the pan, scraping up any brown bits, and add to the lamb mixture. Add 2 cups Chicken Stock, tomatoes, zest, rosemary, thyme, bay leaf, and salt and pepper to taste. Bring the mixture to a boil, cover, and braise in the oven for 2 hours or until lamb is tender and begins to fall off the bone.

Transfer lamb to a shallow platter and keep warm. Remove the zest and bay leaf and discard. Defat the cooking liquid, then reduce over moderately high heat until sauce consistency. Pour over the lamb, sprinkle with parsley, and serve.

PER SERVING

Calories 521	Protein 46.3 grams	Carbohydrate 10.3 grams
Fiber 2.6 grams	Fat 29 grams	Net Carbs 7.7 grams

CHAPTER SEVEN

Poultry

POLLAME

Chicken Romano

Sweet and Sour Chicken Italiano

Grilled Chicken Breasts

Chicken Piccata

Chicken (Pizzaiolo) Pizza Sauce Style

Chicken Caprese

Chicken (Scarpariello) Shoemaker Style

Chicken with Roasted Peppers

Lemon Roast Chicken

Chicken Involtino

Chicken and Mushrooms

Chicken Cutlets

Braised Chicken and Leeks

Chicken in Walnut Sauce

Oven Braised Chicken

Chicken Stuffed with Ham and Cheese

Chicken Marsala

Cornish Game Hen Brick Style

Roasted Cornish Game Hens

Roast Squab

Quail Stuffed with Mushrooms and Herbs

Turkey (Cacciatore) Hunter Style

Turkey with Spinach and Pine Nuts

Turkey Fillets Balsamic

Turkey (Tagliata) Cuts

Seared Turkey Patties with Spinach and Green Sauce

Braised Turkey Legs with Tomatoes and Onions

Roast Duck with Garlic and Shallots

Chicken Romano

Sheepshead Bay, Brooklyn, New York, is renowned for its quaint restaurants.
Years ago I had a delicious version of Chicken Romano (Roman-style chicken)
at Maria's—still there and still owned by the same family since 1932.
Thank God for good things, and some things that never change. If you're
using canned artichokes, make sure they are packed in water, not vinaigrette.

4	chicken breasts, boned with skin on, 6–8 ounces each
	Salt to taste
	Freshly ground black pepper to taste
¼	cup olive oil
2	tablespoons butter
½	medium yellow onion, finely chopped
4	thin slices prosciutto, chopped
2	cloves garlic, minced
8	ounces canned artichoke hearts packed in water, drained and diced
½	cup white wine
1	cup Chicken Stock *(page 61)*
	Juice of ½ lemon
1	cup heavy cream
1	tablespoon chopped fresh Italian Parsley

SERVES 4

Preheat the oven to 400°F.

Season the chicken with salt and pepper. Heat the olive oil in a large ovenproof skillet over moderately high heat. Sear the breasts skin-side down until golden, then turn and put in the oven. Bake until tender and juices no longer run pink, about 15 to 25 minutes depending on the size of the breasts. Transfer the chicken to a warmed platter and keep warm while you prepare the sauce.

To the same pan add the butter and sauté the onion until translucent. Add the prosciutto and garlic and sauté for 1 or 2 minutes, then add the artichokes. Increase the heat and deglaze the pan with the wine, scraping up any brown bits. Add the stock and lemon juice and reduce by half. Add the cream and reduce to thicken. Adjust the seasonings with salt and pepper, then add the parsley and spoon over the finished chicken breasts.

PER SERVING

Calories 794	Protein 47 grams	Carbohydrate 10.5 grams
Fiber 2.4 grams	Fat 60.7 grams	Net Carbs 8.1 grams

Sweet and Sour Chicken Italiano

When we hear "sweet and sour," we think of an Asian-influenced dish, but surprise, this Italian version is habit forming.

1 3½-pound whole chicken, cut into 8 pieces
   Salt to taste
   Freshly ground black pepper to taste
2 tablespoons soy flour for dusting
½ cup extra virgin olive oil, divided
2 small red onions, sliced lengthwise
1 clove garlic, chopped
1 small carrot, finely chopped
1 small celery stalk, finely chopped
2 bay leaves
½ cup white wine
2 cups Chicken Stock *(page 61)*
½ cup balsamic vinegar, divided
2 tablespoons chopped fresh Italian parsley,

SERVES 4

Season the chicken pieces with salt and pepper, then dust with soy flour. Heat ¼ cup of the olive oil in a large skillet with a tight-fitting lid over moderately high heat. Slowly add the chicken pieces, without overcrowding, and brown on all sides. Transfer to a plate and set aside.

In the same skillet, heat the rest of the olive oil and sauté the onions and garlic over moderately high heat for 8 to 10 minutes or until they begin to caramelize. Add the carrot and celery, reduce the heat to low, and cook slowly until the vegetables are softened and golden in color. Increase the heat to moderately high and add the bay leaves and wine. Deglaze the pan, scraping up any brown bits. To the vegetables, add in the chicken pieces, stock, and half of the balsamic vinegar. Adjust the seasoning with salt and pepper, cover, and reduce the heat to low. Simmer for 45 to 60 minutes or until the chicken is very tender. Remove the lid and let liquid reduce for 5 to 8 minutes. Just before serving, discard the bay leaves, add the remaining balsamic vinegar, and sprinkle with parsley.

PER SERVING

Calories 729	Protein 50 grams	Carbohydrate 11 grams
Fiber 1.4 grams	Fat 51 grams	Net Carbs 9.6 grams

Grilled Chicken Breasts

The secret to this delicious chicken is the marinade. And the key to successful prepara-tion is knowing how and when to cook with indirect heat—not a blazing fire.

4	chicken breasts, boned, skinless, 6–8 ounces each,
½	cup extra virgin olive oil
	Juice of 1 lemon
2	cloves garlic, thinly sliced
1	tablespoon chopped fresh Italian parsley
1	tablespoon chopped fresh basil or
	1 teaspoon dried basil
1	tablespoon chopped fresh rosemary or
	1 teaspoon dried rosemary
1	tablespoon chopped fresh thyme or
	1 teaspoon dried thyme
1	tablespoon chopped fresh sage or
	1 teaspoon dried sage
1	teaspoon lemon zest
	Salt to taste
	Freshly ground black pepper to taste

SERVES 4

In a shallow dish, combine the olive oil, lemon juice, garlic, parsley, basil, rosemary, thyme, sage, zest, salt, and pepper. Add chicken and stir to coat well, cover, and chill at least 8 hours.

Preheat the grill. Remove the chicken from the refrigerator and let sit at room temperature for 30 minutes. Pat lightly with paper towels to remove excess oil. Grill the breasts on one side for 10 minutes, turn, and continue to cook for 8 to 10 minutes or until the center is no longer pink. Serve warm or chilled.

PER SERVING

Calories 349	Protein 53.4 grams	Carbohydrate .59 grams
Fiber .15 grams	Fat 13.3 grams	Net Carbs .44 grams

Chicken Piccata

I've added a little more chicken to the ingredients of this Italian favorite because if you're like I am, when you're frying the chicken and sipping your wine, you're going to nibble. Do I know you?

1½–2 pounds chicken cutlets, pounded thin
½ cup soy flour
1 tablespoon extra virgin olive oil
¼ cup butter
¾ cup dry white wine
½ cup fresh lemon juice (about 3 lemons)
1 teaspoon grated lemon zest
⅛ teaspoon dried sage or
  ½ teaspoon chopped fresh sage
¼ teaspoon white pepper
  Salt to taste *(optional)*
1 tablespoon small capers, drained
1 lemon, thinly sliced
2 tablespoons chopped fresh Italian parsley

SERVES 4

Dust the cutlets lightly with the soy flour. Heat the olive oil and butter in a large skillet, sauté chicken cutlets on both sides until thoroughly cooked, and remove to a heated platter.

Add the wine to the skillet and stir over medium to high heat. Add the lemon juice, lemon zest, sage, pepper, salt, and capers.

Continue stirring until the sauce is reduced. The lemon flavor should be the most pronounced; if it is not, add more lemon juice.

Turn off the heat and return the chicken cutlets to the skillet long enough to bathe in the lemon sauce. Arrange the chicken on a warmed serving platter or individual plates.

Garnish the platter or plates with lemon slices and sprinkle parsley over all.

PER SERVING

Calories 430	Protein 44.4 grams	Carbohydrate 6.8 grams
Fiber 1.4 grams	Fat 21.7 grams	Net Carbs 5.4 grams

Variation: For **LAMB PICCATA,** substitute 4–8-ounce shoulder blade chops (boned), pounded thin, in place of chicken. Follow recipe.

PER SERVING

Calories 560	Protein 48.2 grams	Carbohydrate 6.8 grams
Fiber 1.4 grams	Fat 34.4 grams	Net Carbs 5.4 grams

Chicken Pizzaiolo
Pizza Sauce Style

After crisscrossing between cities in North Queensland, Australia, we settled into a seaside hotel and I'd been eating lamb every other night, my favorite, fish, on the other nights. Although I did eat kangaroo, no, it did not taste like chicken. Well, here the menu had chicken pizzaiolo, and as it turned out, the chef had recently moved there from Italy. I decided to try it. This simple meal was exquisite.

4	boneless chicken breasts, 6–8 ounces each
6	tablespoons olive oil
1	small yellow onion, diced
4	ounces button mushrooms, sliced
½	cup white wine
1	cup Tomato Sauce *(page 80)*
¼	teaspoon dried oregano or
	1 teaspoon chopped fresh oregano
	Salt to taste
	Freshly ground black pepper to taste
1	tablespoon chopped fresh Italian parsley

SERVES 4

In a medium skillet, heat 4 tablespoons of the olive oil over moderately high heat and sauté the onion until translucent, about 5 minutes. Add the mushrooms, increase the heat, and brown lightly. Deglaze the skillet with wine; add the Tomato Sauce, oregano, and salt and pepper to taste. Reduce the heat to low and simmer 20 minutes.

Season the chicken with salt and pepper. In a large nonstick skillet, heat the remaining 2 tablespoons of olive oil and brown the chicken on one side. Turn, reduce heat to moderate, and continue cooking until the center is no longer pink. Transfer chicken to a plate and smother with the pizzaiolo sauce. Sprinkle with parsley and serve.

PER SERVING

Calories 469	Protein 41.7 grams	Carbohydrate 5.9 grams
Fiber 1.4 grams	Fat 28.5 grams	Net Carbs 4.5 grams

Chicken Caprese

The style of Capri is represented here, and this sun-drenched island is a lively mix of what's happening with a "cosmo" flair.

4   chicken breasts, boned, with skin (about 8 ounces each)
½   cup commercially prepared roasted red
      peppers, drained and chopped
5   tablespoons freshly squeezed lemon juice, divided
3   teaspoons chopped garlic, divided
      Salt to taste
      Freshly ground black pepper to taste
¾   cup olive oil, divided
1   cup diced fresh mozzarella
1   cup diced plum tomatoes
3   tablespoons finely chopped fresh basil leaves
      or 1 tablespoon dried basil, divided

SERVES 4

In the jar of a blender, combine the red peppers, 4 tablespoons of the lemon juice, 2 teaspoons of the garlic, salt, and pepper and blend until smooth. With the motor running, gradually add ½ cup of the olive oil in a thin stream, stopping to scrape down the sides once or twice. Put the chicken in a nonreactive bowl, add the red pepper mixture, and toss to coat. Marinate in the refrigerator for at least 1 hour.

Meanwhile, prepare the caprese topping. In a medium bowl, combine the tomatoes, mozzarella, remaining olive oil and lemon juice, 2 tablespoons of the basil, remaining garlic, and salt and pepper. Stir well to combine, cover, and let rest at room temperature, stirring occasionally.

Preheat the broiler. Put a broiler pan fitted with wire rack or grill under the broiler until hot. Drain the chicken and place on the hot grill, skin-side down. Broil until the chicken browns and begins to get firm, about 10 minutes. Turn the pieces over and continue to cook until browned, firm, and juices run clear, 8 to 10 minutes more. Transfer the chicken to a warm ovenproof platter and spoon the tomato mixture over it. Put the platter under broiler until the topping is hot and mozzarella just begins to melt; do not brown. Sprinkle with the remaining tablespoon of basil and serve immediately.

PER SERVING

Calories 740	Protein 69 grams	Carbohydrate 4.2 grams
Fiber .52 grams	Fat 47.8 grams	Net Carbs 3.7 grams

Chicken (Scarpariello) Shoemaker Style

It's probably interesting how this "shoemaker recipe" came to be. It has been a Love Chef favorite forever. Please be sure the sausages are butcher quality.

¼	cup extra virgin olive oil
2	tablespoons butter
4	whole cloves garlic
1	pound boneless chicken, cut into bite-sized pieces
1	pound Italian sweet sausages, cut into bite-sized pieces
¼	teaspoon dried oregano or ¾ teaspoon chopped fresh oregano
	Pinch of crushed red pepper flakes
	Salt to taste
	Freshly ground black pepper
¾	cup dry white wine
2	tablespoons fresh Italian parsley, chopped

SERVES 4

In a large skillet, heat olive oil and butter; add garlic. Sauté chicken and sausages, turning frequently until deep golden brown and cooked through. Add spices, salt and pepper, and wine, and reduce liquid slightly. Sprinkle with parsley before serving.

PER SERVING

Calories 735	Protein 48.9 grams	Carbohydrate 3.3 grams
Fiber .17 grams	Fat 54.3 grams	Net Carbs 3.1 grams

Chicken with Roasted Peppers

Buying a prepared product/jarred roasted peppers is a case in point. This recipe is just as good as if you had taken the time to do the peppers yourself. Stock up on them, they are a real time saver.

MAIN DISH

4   chicken breasts, boned, skinless,
        6–8 ounces each
1   7-ounce jar drained roasted peppers—
        cut 8 strips about 3 inches by 1 inch strips
        (reserve remainder for the sauce)
1   medium yellow onion, sliced
        (reserve 1 tablespoon, chopped, for sauce)
    Salt and freshly ground black pepper to taste
¼   cup fresh Italian parsley, chopped
1   tablespoon grated Parmesan cheese
½   teaspoon dried oregano or
        1½ teaspoons chopped fresh oregano
    Olive oil for frying
½   cup Chicken Stock *(page 61)*

SAUCE

Reserved roasted peppers
½ cup Chicken Stock *(page 61)*
½ teaspoon dried oregano or
        1½ teaspoons fresh oregano
1   teaspoon grated Parmesan cheese
1   tablespoon chopped yellow onion
Salt and freshly ground black pepper

SERVES 4 AS A MAIN DISH

Pound chicken breasts until thin. Place 2 pieces of roasted pepper at one end of each piece of chicken; add onion slices, salt, pepper, and parsley and sprinkle with cheese and oregano. Roll in jelly roll style, wrap tightly in wax paper, and refrigerate for 30 minutes.

In a food processor or blender, mix sauce ingredients until smooth, then simmer in a saucepan until thickened.

In a large skillet, sauté chicken rolls in oil until golden; add ½ cup Chicken Stock, cover, and reduce heat. Cook for approximately 35 to 40 minutes. Remove chicken to heated platter.

Cut chicken into pinwheel slices, drizzle with sauce, and serve.

PER SERVING

Calories 493	Protein 64.8 grams	Carbohydrate 5.3 grams
Fiber 1.1 grams	Fat 22 grams	Net Carbs 4.2 grams

Lemon Roast Chicken

There's a famous "little" Italian restaurant in New York City that never has room for you—where the diners love their lemon chicken. Well my friends, I have room for you and here's my version of lemon chicken. (Remember, use only the yellow zest part of the lemon rind for intensive flavor; do not include the white part, which is bitter.)

1	roasting chicken, about 3 pounds
8	tablespoons extra virgin olive oil, divided
4	cloves garlic, chopped
	Zest of 1 lemon
2	tablespoons minced fresh rosemary or 2 teaspoons dried rosemary
2	tablespoons minced fresh sage or 2 teaspoons dried sage
2	teaspoons salt
2	teaspoons freshly ground black pepper
1	tablespoon butter
1	tablespoon shallots
½	cup white wine
1	cup Chicken Stock *(page 61)*

SERVES 4

Preheat the oven to 425°F. Pat the chicken dry with paper towels. In a small bowl, combine 7 tablespoons of the olive oil with the garlic, zest, rosemary, sage, salt, and pepper. Rub mixture over all surfaces of the chicken, both inside and out. Put the chicken on a rack in a roasting pan and add the remaining tablespoon of olive oil and the butter.

Roast the chicken 15 minutes, then reduce heat to 375°F and roast for 20 minutes more.

Reduce the heat again to 325°F for another 15 minutes or until the skin is golden brown and juices from the thigh run clear. Remove from the oven and let rest for 15 minutes to complete cooking.

Cut the chicken into portions, arrange on a heated platter, and keep warm. Drain excess fat from the roasting pan, then heat it over moderately high heat. Add the shallots and sauté until softened. Deglaze the pan with wine, scraping any brown bits from the bottom, and reduce slightly. Add the stock and reduce by half, adjust seasoning with salt and pepper, and pour over chicken to moisten.

PER SERVING

Calories 696	Protein 46.4 grams	Carbohydrate 3.3 grams
Fiber .67 grams	Fat 52.5 grams	Net Carbs 2.6 grams

Chicken (Involtino) Rolled

Of all the cities and regions I have visited in Italy, there was this little "Brooklyn, New York" restaurant long gone that Mr. Alfredo presided over, and this dish was one of my favorites (involtino literally means "rolled," but this version tastes just great). Of course, there were others we'll visit later!

4	chicken breasts, skinned and boned, 6–8 ounces each
2	ounces extra virgin olive oil
½	cup white wine
½	medium red bell pepper, sliced
1	cup spinach leaves
4	slices mozzarella cheese
1	tablespoon butter
	Salt to taste
	Freshly ground black pepper
¼	teaspoon dried thyme or ¾ teaspoon chopped fresh thyme

SERVES 4

Cut pocket in chicken breasts.

Heat olive oil in large skillet; add pepper slices and chicken breasts. Brown chicken breasts on both sides and then remove chicken breasts and peppers from skillet. Divide sautéed peppers and spinach leaves, stuff into pockets of chicken breasts, and add mozzarella.

Meanwhile, add the wine to the skillet, scraping the bottom of the pan, then add butter, salt, pepper, and thyme.

Return chicken breasts to skillet, cover, and continue cooking on low heat for approximately 20 to 25 minutes or until cooked thoroughly.

PER SERVING

Calories 462	Protein 45.9 grams	Carbohydrate 1.8 grams
Fiber .42 grams	Fat 27.2 grams	Net Carbs 1.4 grams

Chicken and Mushrooms

Not to be outdone by Aunt Ida (see page 183), Aunt Rose (from Pop's side of the family) made sure her Chicken and Mushrooms recipe got printed, too. Aunt Rose made this dish for years to feed everyone in her three-family house. I remember eating it in my childhood. Here it is for you to enjoy and pass on to your brood.

8	chicken cutlets, sliced thin
½	cup soy flour
2	tablespoons butter
2	tablespoons extra virgin olive oil
8	ounces white mushrooms, whole caps only
½	medium red bell pepper, cut into matchsticks
1	cup heavy cream
¼	teaspoon white pepper
¼	teaspoon dried sage or 1 teaspoon chopped fresh sage
	Salt to taste
	Fresh Italian parsley for garnish

SERVES 4

Dust the chicken with soy flour. Heat the butter and olive oil in a large skillet and sauté the cutlets until brown and cooked. Remove cutlets to a warm platter.

Add mushrooms and bell pepper and cook until tender. Then add cream, white pepper, sage, and salt; reduce sauce. Spoon over servings of chicken cutlets and garnish with parsley. Serve.

PER SERVING

Calories 563	Protein 41.4 grams	Carbohydrate 8.5 grams
Fiber 2 grams	Fat 40.9 grams	Net Carbs 6.5 grams

Chicken Cutlets

*I created this recipe for my Uncle Vinnie, and these chicken cutlets are
unlike any you have ever tasted. The name of the recipe sounds traditional,
but a look at the ingredients list will tell you otherwise. Uncle Vinnie was
in heaven (where he now resides permanently) when he ate these cutlets.
Uncle Vinnie, this recipe is printed in your memory.*

8 chicken cutlets, sliced thin
1 large egg, lightly beaten
¼ cup half-and-half
2 tablespoons grated Parmesan cheese
1 tablespoon chopped fresh Italian parsley
¼ teaspoon white pepper
   Salt to taste *(optional)*
1 cup soy flour
3 tablespoons extra virgin olive oil

SERVES 4

Pound the cutlets thin. In a shallow bowl, mix the egg, half-and-half,
cheese, parsley, pepper, and salt. Dip the cutlets into the mixture, then
press into the soy flour.

In a large skillet, sauté the cutlets in the olive oil until golden
brown and cooked.

PER SERVING

Calories 416	Protein 45.5 grams	Carbohydrate 7.7 grams
Fiber 2.1 grams	Fat 22 grams	Net Carbs 000 grams

Variation: For **Alla Parmigiana**—Add slices of mozzarella cheese (8
ounces) to finished cutlet and bake at 375°F for 20 minutes. Top with
1½ cups marinara sauce. Serve.

PER SERVING

Calories 639	Protein 57.4 grams	Carbohydrate 13.3 grams
Fiber 3.2 grams	Fat 39.5 grams	Net Carbs 10.1 grams

Braised Chicken and Leeks

*This dish is what I consider to be a perfect dish. I know you'll want to sneak
in two chicken legs per person, but with a salad and low-carb vegetables,
you really don't need to. Try to get the large size oven roaster chicken legs.
If you can find only the smaller legs and thighs, then serve two per person.*

4	large chicken legs with thigh meat, cut in half
	Salt to taste
	Freshly ground black pepper to taste
½	cup extra virgin olive oil, divided
¾	cup yellow onion, diced
2	medium leeks split, diced
2	cloves garlic, minced
½	cup white wine
2	cups Chicken Stock *(page 61)*
4	bay leaves

SERVES 4

Preheat the oven to 350°F. Season the chicken legs with salt and pepper. Heat ¼ cup of the olive oil over moderately high heat in a nonstick skillet and brown the chicken pieces on all sides. Arrange the chicken in a single layer in a shallow pan or heatproof dish and set aside.

In the same skillet, heat the remaining olive oil over moderate heat and sauté the onion, leeks, and garlic until onion is golden, about 8 minutes. Add the wine and deglaze the pan, scraping up any brown bits. Add the Chicken Stock, bay leaves, salt, and pepper.

Cover and bake in the oven for one hour or until the chicken is very tender. Discard bay leaves before serving.

PER SERVING

Calories 717	Protein 48.1 grams	Carbohydrate 10.1 grams
Fiber 1.4 grams	Fat 51 grams	Net Carbs 8.7 grams

Chicken in Walnut Sauce

*I once spent a memorable New Year's Eve in Monte Carlo, on my way by auto
to Milan with an overnight stop in Genoa. I arrived in Genoa at night in the
bustling waterfront area, where ships and sailors the world over pass through.
Settling in the hotel, I was anxious to find a good meal. "No problem," said the hotel
manager, who called a cab, and I drove away from the waterfront. Don't ask, I can't
remember the restaurant's name, but I'll never forget the heavenly Walnut Sauce.*

4	halved chicken breasts, with skin and bones
	Salt to taste
	Freshly ground black pepper
2	tablespoons soy flour
2	tablespoons butter
2	tablespoons extra virgin olive oil
½	pound sliced white mushrooms
2	scallions, chopped
1	cup Chicken Stock *(page 61)*
2	tablespoons chopped fresh Italian parsley
1	teaspoon chopped fresh thyme or
	a pinch of dried thyme
½	cup sour cream
½	cup ground walnuts, toasted *(see page 28)*

SERVES 4

Season the chicken with salt and pepper then sprinkle with flour and
toss to coat. In a deep skillet, heat the butter and olive oil over moderately high heat and brown the breasts on both sides. Add the mushrooms, scallions, stock, parsley, thyme, and salt and pepper. Bring the
mixture to a boil, then cover; reduce heat to low and simmer 25 to 30
minutes or until chicken has no traces of pink inside.

Transfer the breasts to a warmed serving platter and keep warm.
Add the sour cream and walnuts to the skillet and heat through without boiling. Pour the sauce over the chicken and serve.

PER SERVING

Calories 364	Protein 20 grams	Carbohydrate 6.4 grams
Fiber 1.8 grams	Fat 29 grams	Net Carbs 4.6 grams

Oven Braised Chicken

*I remember this as my Aunt Ida's (Pop's sister) recipe. They (and their
other five brothers) swear that this recipe remains unchanged and that it
was actually passed down from Grandma. Who knows? All I know is that it's
tasty and can be doubled or tripled to feed a crowd (or a very large family).*

1	3- to 4-pound chicken, cut into 8 pieces
	Salt to taste
	Freshly ground black pepper to taste
	Soy flour for dusting
¼–½	cup extra virgin olive oil, divided
1	medium yellow onion, sliced
2	cloves garlic, chopped
2	bay leaves
2	teaspoons fresh chopped rosemary
	or ¾ teaspoon dried rosemary
½	cup white wine
2	fresh plum tomatoes, chopped
2	cups Chicken Stock *(page 61)*

SERVES 4

Preheat the oven to 350°. Season the chicken with salt and pepper.
Dust with soy flour and toss to coat. In a large heavy skillet, heat ½
the olive oil over moderately high heat. Brown the chicken in batches,
being careful not to overcrowd the skillet. As the chicken browns,
transfer the pieces, skin-side up, to a Dutch oven or large heavy
saucepan with a tight-fitting lid and set aside.

Add some fresh olive oil to the skillet if necessary, and sauté the
onion until translucent, 5 to 8 minutes. Add the garlic, bay leaves, and
rosemary and sauté for 1 minute. Add the wine, deglazing the pan and
scraping up any brown bits, and reduce slightly. Add this mixture to
the chicken along with the tomatoes, stock, salt, and pepper. Bring the
chicken mixture to a boil, cover, and transfer immediately to the oven.
Braise the chicken until it almost falls off the bone, 45 to 60 minutes.
Discard bay leaves before serving.

PER SERVING

Calories 691	Protein 55.3 grams	Carbohydrate 5.2 grams
Fiber .92 grams	Fat 46.7 grams	Net Carbs 4.3 grams

Chicken Stuffed with Ham and Cheese

Chicken Italian style. After visiting St. Francis of Assisi when in Sienna, we were motoring and stopped for lunch at an Autogrill on the Autostrade. This is the quality of food served along the Italian highway. Real slow food, Italian style.

4	boneless and skinless chicken breasts, 6–8 ounces each
6	eggs
1	tablespoon chopped fresh Italian parsley
1	teaspoon minced fresh rosemary or a pinch of dried rosemary
	Salt to taste
	Freshly ground black pepper to taste
2	tablespoons olive oil, plus a little for cooking the eggs
8	tablespoons grated Parmesan cheese
4	slices ham
8	tablespoons grated mozzarella cheese
2	tablespoons butter
½	cup white wine
½	cup Chicken Stock *(page 61)*

SERVES 4

To prepare the chicken breasts, begin cutting with a sharp knife lengthwise along the thicker side of each breast. Keeping the knife level with the work surface, carefully work your way to the straight side, cutting three-quarters of the way through. Open the breast and lay it flat on a piece of plastic, then cover with another piece of plastic. Using a meat mallet, pound the breast until thin. Store in the refrigerator until ready to use.

For the filling, whisk the eggs, parsley, rosemary, salt, and pepper together in a small bowl. Heat enough olive oil to lightly coat the skillet, then pour in the egg mixture. Cook, lifting edges to permit uncooked egg mixture to flow to the bottom, until set. Carefully turn over and cook until just set on the bottom. Cut the omelet into 4 equal portions and set aside to cool.

To assemble the rolls, remove the top layer of plastic from one of the breasts, season with salt and pepper, then sprinkle with 2 tablespoons of the Parmesan. Put a portion of the omelet in the center of the breast, then top with a slice of ham and sprinkle with 2 tablespoons of the mozzarella. Starting on one long side, roll the chicken breast and secure with toothpicks or kitchen twine. Cover and chill until ready to serve.

Sprinkle the rolls with salt and pepper. In a large skillet, heat the butter and 2 tablespoons of olive oil over moderately high heat and sear the rolls until golden on all sides. Add the wine and deglaze the pan, scraping up brown bits; then add the stock, salt, and pepper. Reduce the heat to low, cover, and cook the rolls for about 20 minutes, turning occasionally until the breasts are firm to the touch but not dry. Remove the toothpicks or twine and slice each roll on an angle about one inch thick. Arrange fanned on a warmed serving platter and keep warm. Reduce the liquid in the skillet by half and drizzle over the rolls to moisten.

PER SERVING

Calories 559	Protein 58.8 grams	Carbohydrate 2 grams
Fiber .06 grams	Fat 31.7 grams	Net Carbs 1.9 grams

Chicken Marsala

Marsala is a Sicilian dessert wine with a distinctive taste of burned sugar. Available dry (which is sweet) and sweet (which is sweeter). You want the dry for this recipe.

4   large chicken cutlets
    Soy flour, approximately ½ cup
      (or more if needed)
1   tablespoon extra virgin olive oil
3   tablespoons butter
¾   cup dry Marsala
¼   teaspoon white pepper
    Salt to taste (*optional*)
⅛   teaspoon grated nutmeg

SERVES 4

Pound the cutlets thin and dust lightly with the soy flour. In a medium skillet, gently sauté the cutlets in the olive oil and butter until cooked. Remove to a warm platter. Add the Marsala, pepper, salt, and nutmeg to the skillet. Cook over high heat, stirring constantly until thickened. Remove from the heat.

Return the chicken cutlets to the skillet to bathe in the sauce. Serve.

PER SERVING

Calories 403	Protein 38.5 grams	Carbohydrate 8.8 grams
Fiber 1.1 grams	Fat 18.2 grams	Net Carbs 7.7 grams

Cornish Game Hen (Brick Style)

Cornish game hens intrigued my mother, who would stuff them
sometimes, otherwise she would let Pop grill them, weighing them
down with his foil-covered bricks. I've suggested an alternative to
Dad's bricks, but if you prefer his method, by all means try it.

4	Cornish game hens
½	cup olive oil, divided
1	tablespoon red pepper flakes
2	teaspoons freshly ground black pepper
2	teaspoons dried oregano
	or 2 tablespoons chopped fresh oregano
1	teaspoon salt

SERVES 4

Using a sharp knife, hold one of the game hens upright by the breast and cut down both sides of the backbone, removing it completely. Lay the bird breast-side down on the work surface and spread the bird open, exposing the inside. Press the bird flat and make a slice in the breastbone. Pull the wings to the side and tuck backward to hold in place. Repeat with the remaining game hens. Rub both sides of the game hen with 1 tablespoon of the olive oil, then sprinkle with the pepper flakes, pepper, oregano, and salt. Cover and marinate in the refrigerator for at least 1 hour.

Preheat the oven to 400°F. Heat the remaining olive oil in a large heavy skillet over moderately high heat. Put 2 game hens in the skillet skin side-down and place a heavy shallow pan on top of the birds. Fill another saucepan with water, cover tightly, and put in the shallow pan, weighing and pressing the game hens down. Sear until a deep, golden brown, then turn and brown the other side. Transfer the game hens to a baking sheet and keep warm while searing the remaining game hens. Cook the game hens on the baking sheet in the oven for 8 to 12 minutes, or until very tender.

PER SERVING

Calories 1044	Protein 68.5 grams	Carbohydrate 1.9 grams
Fiber .97 grams	Fat 83 grams	Net Carbs .9 grams

Roasted Cornish Game Hens

Here's another recipe that was inspired by my mom. Perhaps it was the fact that while the hens were in the oven, she could fix all the other courses.

4	Cornish game hens
¼	cup olive oil
	Salt to taste
	Freshly ground black pepper to taste
8	cloves garlic, minced
1	medium yellow onion, quartered
2	lemons, quartered
4	sprigs rosemary or 1 teaspoon dried rosemary
4	sprigs thyme or 1 teaspoon dried thyme
4	sprigs sage or 1 teaspoon dried sage

SERVES 4

Preheat the oven to 400°F. Wash the game hens inside and out and pat dry with paper towels. Rub the game hens with the olive oil and season with the salt and pepper and herbs. Rub the cavity of the game hen with the garlic; then divide the onion and lemon quarters equally among the 4 birds. Roast the game hens for 30 to 40 minutes or until juices run clear when the thigh is pierced with a small sharp knife.

PER SERVING

Calories 924	Protein 68.5 grams	Carbohydrate 2 grams
Fiber .13 grams	Fat 69.3 grams	Net Carbs 1.9 grams

Roast Squab

Here's another dish that I enjoyed at the Savoy Hotel in Florence.
Even though I'm not a squab lover, this was such a grand lunch that
I didn't care if my dinner that night was "bird size."

4	squab, 6–8 ounces each
¼	cup olive oil
	Salt to taste
	Freshly ground black pepper to taste
2	teaspoons chopped fresh thyme or
	¾ teaspoon dried thyme
2	teaspoons chopped fresh rosemary or
	¾ teaspoon dried rosemary
2	tablespoons butter
1	small yellow onion, chopped
1	clove garlic, minced
2	slices ham, chopped
2	slices prosciutto, chopped
2	teaspoons chopped fresh sage or
	1 teaspoon dried sage
½	cup white wine
1½	cups Chicken Stock *(page 61)* or
	1½ cups canned chicken stock
1	tablespoon chopped fresh Italian parsley

SERVES 4

Preheat the oven to 375°F.

Rub the squab with the olive oil and season inside and out with salt and pepper. Sprinkle the squab with the thyme and rosemary and roast in a 375°F oven for 30 minutes.

Meanwhile, prepare the sauce. In a small skillet, melt the butter over moderate heat. Sauté the onion until golden, 8 to 10 minutes. Add the garlic, ham, prosciutto, and sage and sauté 5 minutes. Deglaze the pan with wine, then add the stock and reduce by half. Serve the sauce with the roast squab and garnish with parsley.

PER SERVING

Calories 812	Protein 41 grams	Carbohydrate 2.6 grams
Fiber .47 grams	Fat 67.8 grams	Net Carbs 2.1 grams

Quail Stuffed with Mushrooms and Herbs

*Have your butcher dress the quail and remove the breastbone and this recipe is
an impressive dinner-party dish. I guarantee it will come out perfetto! If stuffing
is left over, put it in foil, roast it with the quail, and serve it alongside.*

8	quail, breastbone removed
2	tablespoons butter
4	tablespoons olive oil, divided
1	pound button mushrooms, chopped
1	small yellow onion, diced
1	small stalk celery, diced
1	small carrot, diced
2	slices prosciutto, chopped
2	cloves garlic, minced
1	tablespoon chopped fresh Italian parsley
1	teaspoon chopped fresh thyme or a pinch of dried thyme
½	cup white wine
2	egg yolks
2	tablespoons breadcrumbs
	Salt to taste
	Freshly ground black pepper to taste

SERVES 4

In a large skillet, heat the butter and 2 tablespoons of the olive oil over
moderate heat. Add the mushrooms and onion; sauté until onion is
soft. Add the celery and carrot, and cook until all the vegetables are
tender. Increase the heat to moderately high and add the prosciutto,
garlic, parsley, and thyme; sauté for 3 minutes. Deglaze the skillet
with the wine and reduce until dry. Cool the mixture for 5 to 10 minutes. Blend in the yolks and breadcrumbs and season with salt and
pepper. Divide the stuffing evenly among the quail. Season the quail
with salt and pepper, drizzle with the remaining olive oil, and roast for
25 minutes or until very tender. Serve whole.

PER SERVING

Calories 793	Protein 49.4 grams	Carbohydrate 11 grams
Fiber 2.3 grams	Fat 49.2 grams	Net Carbs 8.7 grams

Turkey (Cacciatore) Hunter Style

Years ago I became friendly with the Great Sammy Davis, Jr., and when he was on tour with Frank and Liza in Westchester, New York, I was planning this dish for dinner in his honor after their performance—but it wasn't to be. He apologized because the performance ran late. Unfortunately, he passed away shortly thereafter.

4	turkey fillets, cut into 16 pieces
4	tablespoons extra virgin olive oil, divided
2	cloves garlic
2	small yellow onions, chopped
1	stalk celery, chopped
8	fresh ripe plum tomatoes, chopped
	(or 1 20-ounce can)
2	bay leaves
½	tablespoon dried sage or
	1½ tablespoons chopped fresh sage
1	tablespoon dried rosemary or
	3 tablespoons chopped fresh rosemary
	Freshly ground black pepper to taste
	Salt to taste
1½	cups Chicken Stock (*page 61*)
¾	cup dry red wine
4	ounces whole button mushrooms

Serves 4

In a large skillet, brown the turkey fillets in 2 tablespoons of olive oil. When all the pieces are browned, remove the turkey fillets from the skillet.

In the same skillet, sauté the garlic, onions, and celery in the remaining 2 tablespoons of olive oil until soft; add the tomatoes, bay leaves, sage, rosemary, pepper, and salt. Return the turkey fillets to the skillet, cover, and simmer for 25 to 30 minutes. Add the stock, wine, and mushrooms. Continue to simmer, uncovered, for an additional 30 minutes, until turkey is cooked. Discard bay leaves before serving.

PER SERVING

Calories 488	Protein 63.8 grams	Carbohydrate 12.9 grams
Fiber 3.2 grams	Fat 16.3 grams	Net Carbs 9.7 grams

Turkey with Spinach and Pine Nuts

I'd like to recommend drinking a Bolla Pino Grigio with this dish;
reserving a half cup to use in this recipe would go a long way on flavor.

1	medium yellow onion, diced
6	tablespoons extra virgin olive oil, divided
¼	pound pancetta, thinly sliced and chopped
1	teaspoon dried rosemary or
	1 tablespoon chopped fresh rosemary
2	cloves garlic
½	cup white wine
1½	pounds spinach, washed,
	thoroughly dried, and chopped
½	cup pine nuts, toasted *(see page 28)*
	Salt to taste
	Freshly ground black pepper
1–1¼	pounds turkey breast, cut into 1-inch pieces
2	tablespoons chopped fresh Italian parsley

SERVES 4

In a large skillet, sauté the onion in 2 tablespoons of olive oil until golden. Add the pancetta, rosemary, and garlic and sauté 5 minutes. Add white wine and reduce on low heat. Transfer to a bowl and set aside.

Heat 2 tablespoons of olive oil in the same skillet and sauté the spinach until tender. Add to the onion mixture along with the pine nuts, season with salt and pepper, then set aside.

Wash and dry the skillet. Season the turkey with salt and pepper. Heat the remaining olive oil in the skillet and sauté the turkey in batches until golden brown and thoroughly cooked, transferring the pieces to the spinach mixture when done. When the last batch of turkey is cooked, return the turkey and spinach mixture to the skillet. Add the parsley and heat through.

PER SERVING

Calories 567	Protein 49.4 grams	Carbohydrate 11.8 grams
Fiber 6 grams	Fat 35.1 grams	Net Carbs 5.8 grams

Turkey Fillets Balsamic

A few years ago, neck tags with this now-popular recipe first appeared on Colavita's balsamic vinegar bottles. I've replaced the regular flour with soy flour to make it lower carb.

4	large turkey fillets
2	tablespoons soy flour
	Fresh pepper and salt to taste
¼	cup extra virgin olive oil
1	medium red bell pepper, seeded and cut into strips
4–6	ounces oyster mushrooms, cleaned and torn apart
4	garlic cloves, sliced
½	cup balsamic vinegar
½	cup Chicken Stock (*page 61*)
1	tablespoon Dijon mustard
1	teaspoon dried thyme or 1 tablespoon chopped fresh thyme

IN ADDITION:

1	tablespoon soy flour
2	tablespoons balsamic vinegar

SERVES 4

In a large skillet, heat olive oil.

Mix soy flour with pepper and salt and dust turkey fillets. Sauté turkey fillets about 5 minutes; turn over when brown. Add bell pepper strips, mushrooms, and garlic. Continue cooking another 5 minutes.

Meanwhile, mix balsamic vinegar, chicken stock, mustard, and thyme and add to turkey fillets. Cover and continue to cook for approximately 30 minutes over medium heat. Remove turkey.

Mix 1 tablespoon of flour with 2 tablespoons of balsamic vinegar, add to skillet, stir, and cook 5 to 7 minutes. Return turkey fillets to marry flavors.

PER SERVING

Calories 460	Protein 63.3 grams	Carbohydrate 13 grams
Fiber 2.1 grams	Fat 16.6 grams	Net Carbs 10.9 grams

Turkey (Tagliata) Cuts

Thanksgiving Day last year I was in Ravello on the Amalfi coast. Like you, I always eat turkey on Thanksgiving, but in Italy at dinner I joked with the waiter at the hotel and asked, "Where's the turkey on the menu?" The following night at dinner, the waiter told me, "No menu tonight, the chef has a surprise"—this was it, Turkey Tagliata. (Tagliata is the method used to cut a turkey.)

1¼ pounds turkey breast,
   cut into ¼-inch thick cutlets
½ cup extra virgin olive oil
2 teaspoons dried sage or
   2 tablespoons chopped fresh sage
1 teaspoon lemon zest
   Salt to taste
   Freshly ground black pepper to taste
6 ounces mixed baby greens
   Juice of one lemon

SERVES 4

Pound the cutlets between two pieces of plastic with a meat mallet until they are thin and somewhat transparent. In a small bowl, whisk the olive oil, sage, lemon zest, salt, and pepper. Brush this mixture on the cutlets and refrigerate for 30 to 60 minutes.

Preheat the grill. Grill the cutlets on a hot grill for 1 to 2 minutes; turn and finish cooking, about 1 to 2 more minutes. Transfer to a platter, top with baby greens, drizzle with lemon juice, and adjust seasoning with salt and pepper. May be broiled or pan fried, if preferred.

PER SERVING

Calories 237	Protein 37.7 grams	Carbohydrate 2.6 grams
Fiber .9 grams	Fat 7.8 grams	Net Carbs 1.7 grams

Seared Turkey Patties with Spinach and Green Sauce

*Fresh herbs can make a flavor difference in many dishes, and
in this recipe you'll taste it if you use fresh sage.*

1½	pounds ground turkey
½	cup chopped prosciutto, about 2 ounces
½	cup grated Parmesan cheese
1	egg
2	cloves garlic, minced
2	teaspoons grated lemon zest
2	teaspoons minced fresh sage or
	¾ teaspoon dried sage
	Salt to taste
	Freshly ground black pepper to taste
¼	cup olive oil
	Sautéed Spinach (*page 96*)
¾	cup Green Sauce (*page 78*)

SERVES 4

Preheat the oven to 400°F.

Put the ground turkey in a medium bowl. Add the prosciutto, Parmesan, egg, garlic, zest, sage, salt, and pepper and mix until well combined. Form the mixture into 2-inch balls, flattening them slightly.

In a large ovenproof skillet, heat the olive oil over moderately high heat. Gradually add the patties, being careful not to crowd the pan, and sear until the bottoms are well browned. Do not lift the patty too early or it will stick; if it slides when the pan is shaken, it's safe to turn. Immediately after turning the patty, put the skillet in the oven and continue to cook until the patty is no longer pink inside. Serve on a bed of Sautéed Spinach with Green Sauce on the side.

PER SERVING (MEAT, SPINACH, AND SAUCE)

Calories 885	Protein 48 grams	Carbohydrate 11.3 grams
Fiber 5.3 grams	Fat 73.4 grams	Net Carbs 6 grams

Braised Turkey Legs with Tomatoes and Onions

Turkey legs always have been my favorite when a whole roasted turkey is presented. Today, I don't have to wait for a major holiday because turkey parts are available in most super stores and markets.

½   cup olive oil
4   small to medium turkey legs
    Salt to taste
    Freshly ground black pepper to taste
2   tablespoons soy flour for dusting
2   medium yellow onions, sliced
2   cloves garlic, minced
1   teaspoon red pepper flakes
3   cups Chicken Stock *(page 61)* or
        3 cups canned chicken stock
2   cups Tomato Sauce *(page 80)*
1   bay leaf
2   tablespoons chopped fresh Italian parsley, divided
½   cup scallions, chopped

SERVES 4

Preheat the oven to 350°F. In a large, deep ovenproof skillet with a tight-fitting lid, heat the olive oil over moderately high heat. Season the turkey legs with salt and pepper, then dust with soy flour. Brown each turkey leg until golden, and set aside.

To the same skillet, add the onions and sauté until golden, about 8 minutes. Add the garlic and red pepper flakes and stir 1 minute. Add the stock, Tomato Sauce, 1 tablespoon of the parsley and salt and pepper to taste. Add the bay leaf and turkey legs and bring the liquid to a simmer. Cover and bake in the oven for 1 hour or until turkey is very tender.

Transfer the turkey legs to a warmed serving platter; reduce the cooking liquid by half and pour over the legs. Discard bay leaf. Sprinkle with the scallions and remaining parsley.

PER SERVING

Calories 1529	Protein 159.1 grams	Carbohydrate 13.9 grams
Fiber 3.2 grams	Fat 89.3 grams	Net Carbs 10.7 grams

Roast Duck with Garlic and Shallots

Duck is one food most people don't try to attempt making at home—but try this one because it's easy and it's foolproof. It's also delicious.

1   **whole duck, quartered**
     Salt to taste
     Freshly ground black pepper to taste
1   **tablespoon chopped fresh rosemary or**
       1 teaspoon dried rosemary
1   **tablespoon chopped fresh sage or**
       1 teaspoon dried sage
1   **cup garlic, sliced ⅛ inch thick**
1   **cup shallots, sliced ⅛ inch thick**
1   **tablespoon chopped fresh Italian parsley**

SERVES 4

Preheat the oven to 350°F. Season the duck with salt and pepper. Combine the rosemary and sage in a small dish, then press the mixture into the duck. Arrange the duck pieces on a rack over a roasting pan or baking sheet without crowding. Roast the duck for 1 hour.

Add the garlic and shallots to the pan and stir to coat with drippings. Roast duck 15 minutes more or until juices run clear (not pink) when legs are pierced with a small sharp knife. Transfer the duck to a warmed serving platter and keep warm. Remove the garlic and shallots with a slotted spoon and transfer to a small bowl. Stir in the parsley and adjust seasoning with salt and pepper; sprinkle over the duck pieces. Serve immediately.

PER SERVING
Calories 725   Protein 39.5 grams   Carbohydrate 18.2 grams
Fiber 1.1 grams   Fat 54.4 grams   Net Carbs 17.1 grams

CHAPTER EIGHT

#

DOLCI

Ricotta Parfaits

Sautéed Pears with Rum Sauce

Semifreddo with Coffee and Amaretto

Sicilian Dessert

Strawberries with Almond Meringue

*Cooked Crème (*PANNA COTTA*) with Seasonal Berries*

Coffee Crystals

Chocolate Granita Espresso

Fresh Fruit Tart

Egg Custard

Mom's Cheesecake

*Baked Pudding (*BONET*)*

Goat Cheese and Cherry Ramekins

Almond Ricotta

Ricotta Parfaits

These delicious parfaits can be made before the main entrée—but do not make a day before. Your selection of fruits should be chosen with care for low carbs. As you know, most fruits are high in carbs, with the lowest-carb being fresh kumquats, cranberries, grapefruits, Thompson seedless grapes, passion fruit, and prime watermelon. Ironically, many canned fruits packed in water are lower in carbs than their fresh versions.

1½	cups whole milk ricotta cheese
1	tablespoon honey
2	teaspoons Splenda Granular
3	eggs, separated
½	teaspoon vanilla
1	cup chopped soft fruits, such as fresh, whole berries

SERVES 4

Put the ricotta in a sieve over a bowl. Pressing with a spatula or the back of a ladle, strain it through the sieve. Put the ricotta in the bowl of a food processor, if available, and process until smooth. In the top of a double boiler or a heatproof bowl, combine the ricotta, honey, Splenda, egg yolks, and vanilla. Place the pan or bowl over simmering water and heat through. Set aside to cool.

Beat the egg whites until stiff. Whisk one third of the egg whites into the ricotta mixture then fold in the remaining egg whites. Put some fruit in the bottom of a chilled goblet, top with ¼ of the ricotta mixture, and top with fruit. Chill and serve immediately.

PER SERVING

Calories 260	Protein 15.5 grams	Carbohydrate 13.1 grams
Fiber 1.1 grams	Fat 16.2 grams	Net Carbs 11.7 grams

Sautéed Pears with Rum Sauce

Using canned rather than fresh pears here results in a lower carb count.

3	egg yolks
¾	cup heavy cream
½	cup Splenda Granular, divided
5	teaspoons dark rum
1	teaspoon vanilla
	Juice of ½ lemon
3	tablespoons butter
1	15-ounce can pears packed in water (do not use fresh)
¼	cup raisins
1	teaspoon grated lemon zest
⅛	teaspoon grated nutmeg
	Optional: 2 tablespoons coarsely chopped toasted walnuts (will add additional carbs)

SERVES 4

Prepare a medium-sized bowl with ice water. In the top of a double boiler or a heatproof bowl, combine the yolks, cream, and ¼ cup Splenda. Set the pan or bowl over a pan of simmering water and cook, stirring frequently, until the sauce thickens enough to coat a spoon, 20 to 30 minutes. Do not boil. Remove the pan or bowl from the hot water, set into the ice water and stir in the rum, vanilla, and lemon juice. Cool thoroughly, then chill.

When you are ready to serve, heat the butter in a large heavy skillet over moderate heat. Add the pears, raisins, remaining Splenda, and zest and sauté until tender but not mushy, about 3 to 5 minutes. Stir in nutmeg, then divide among 4 dessert plates. Pour the chilled sauce over the pear mixture and sprinkle with walnuts if desired.

PER SERVING

Calories 358	Protein 3.7 grams	Carbohydrate 20 grams
Fiber 2.2 grams	Fat 29.1 grams	Net Carbs 16.7 grams

Semifreddo with Coffee and Amaretto

This delicious "cold creamy dessert" is one of many called a semiffredo in Italy. Amaretto is the liqueur of choice, but you may have a favorite flavor—maybe even not Italian.

8	eggs, separated
1	cup Splenda Granular
2	cups heavy cream
¼	cup strong, cold espresso
¼	cup Amaretto
½	cup sliced almonds, chopped

SERVES 4

In the bowl of a mixer, whip the egg yolks with the Splenda until they have tripled in volume and are light and lemon colored. Transfer to a large bowl and set aside. Wash and dry the mixing bowl, then add the cream and whip until peaks begin to form but are not stiff. Add egg yolk mixture and chill thoroughly. Wash and dry the mixing bowl. Whip the egg whites until stiff and shiny. Gently fold the egg whites into the cream mixture and put half of this mixture in another bowl. Add espresso to one bowl and gently fold in; then add the Amaretto to the other bowl and fold in the almonds.

In a 9-inch metal loaf pan lined completely with plastic wrap, pour the espresso mixture into the pan; then top with the Amaretto mixture. Cover with plastic wrap and freeze until firm.

To unmold the semifreddo, dip the pan in a hot water bath for 3 to 5 seconds, then invert onto a serving platter. Unwrap, slice; and serve immediately.

PER SERVING

Calories 712	Protein 17.5 grams	Carbohydrate 19.2 grams
Fiber 1.2 grams	Fat 60.1 grams	Net Carbs 12.5 grams

Sicilian Dessert

Sitting in the Piazza Duomo in Syracuse, Sicily, enjoying my Cassata Siciliana while watching the strolling Italians, prompted me to include this famous Sicilian dessert in this book. Its taste is as true as I can get.

2	cups whole milk ricotta cheese
⅓	cup Splenda Granular, divided
1	cup heavy cream, whipped and chilled
¼	cup grated orange peel (or candied orange peel, chopped)
8	tablespoons unsweetened baker's chocolate, grated
¼	cup finely chopped pistachios
¼	teaspoon nutmeg
1	ounce dark rum or brandy
1	ounce orange liqueur
6	slices low-carb bread, crusts trimmed*
1	tablespoon powdered sugar for dusting

SERVES 8

In a bowl, whisk together the ricotta cheese and ¼ cup of Splenda. Add the cream and whisk until smooth. Fold in the orange peel, all but 1 tablespoon of the chocolate, the pistachios, and the nutmeg. Cover and chill.

Line a small loaf pan completely with plastic wrap. In a small bowl, combine the rum and orange liqueur. Cut each slice of low-carb bread into 3 strips and brush lightly with the rum mixture. Arrange half of the bread strips in the bottom of the pan and spread half of the ricotta mixture over them. Repeat this procedure, ending with a layer of bread strips. Wrap the cassata tightly and refrigerate.

To serve, unwrap the cassata and invert onto a serving dish. Remove the plastic and dust with the powdered sugar. Sprinkle with the remaining chocolate and slice to serve.

*NOTE: low-carb bread averages 3.4 to 5 carbs per slice, a great substitution for cake.

PER SERVING

Calories 358	Protein 14.6 grams	Carbohydrate 15.4 grams
Fiber 5 grams	Fat 27 grams	Net Carbs 9.6 grams

Amaretto Strawberries with Almond Meringue

*This is a favorite dish of my friend Joyce Randolph (Trixie of
The Honeymooners), and I'm sure after you taste it, you'll love it, too.*

4	cups sliced strawberries, room temperature
¼	cup Splenda Granular, plus ⅓ teaspoon, depending on sweetness of strawberries
2	tablespoons Amaretto
4	egg whites
	Pinch of cream of tartar
½	tablespoon almonds, chopped and toasted *(see page 28)*

SERVES 4

Preheat the oven to 450°F.

Slice the strawberries and put in a shallow 9-inch pie pan. Sprinkle with ⅓ teaspoon Splenda and Amaretto and toss to coat. Set aside. (*Option:* Add a teaspoon of cornstarch at this stage to compensate for the juice from the strawberries. You'll also be adding carbs.)

In the bowl of a mixer, combine the egg whites and cream of tartar, and beat on high speed until foamy. With the motor running, slowly add ¼ cup of the Splenda, scraping the bowl once or twice, until stiff peaks form. Gently fold in the chopped almonds and spread the meringue over the strawberries. Bake 5 minutes, or until the top is golden brown. Serve immediately.

PER SERVING

Calories 110	Protein 4.7 grams	Carbohydrate 18.9 grams
Fiber 3.9 grams	Fat 1 gram	Net Carbs 00 grams

Cooked Crème with Seasonal Berries

PANNA COTTA

I found a great way to enjoy this traditional Italian dessert from Piedmont without the carbs, by substituting Splenda—now it's guilt free!

2   cups heavy cream
2   tablespoons grated orange zest
1   cup half-and-half
1   envelope gelatin
6   tablespoons Splenda Granular
Option: Choose berries for garnish; watch extra carbs.

SERVES 4

Combine the cream and zest in a 1-quart saucepan and heat over moderately low heat. Heat the cream, tasting occasionally, until the cream is infused with orange flavor. Strain and set aside.

To the saucepan, add the half-and-half and heat to scalding. Gradually whisk in the gelatin; add the Splenda and stir until dissolved. Remove from heat and add the infused cream. Divide the mixture among four 1-cup custard cups or ramekins and chill until set.

To unmold, put the cups or ramekins in hot water for 10 seconds, run a knife along the edge, and then turn out onto individual dessert plates. Garnish with berries, if desired. Serve.

PER SERVING

Calories 508	Protein 6 grams	Carbohydrate 8.3 grams
Fiber .32 grams	Fat 50 grams	Net Carbs 6 grams

Coffee Crystals

This is a sweet treat that is sure to please. Serve it on a hot evening or afternoon and watch for the smiles. Use your favorite coffee blend.

2   cups freshly brewed double-strength coffee
3   tablespoons Splenda Granular
4   lemon twists

SERVES 4

While the coffee is still hot, add the Splenda and stir until dissolved. Chill thoroughly. Pour the sweetened coffee into a 9-inch shallow pan to a depth of less than 1 inch. Put the pan in the freezer for 1 hour. Gently stir the ice crystals to mix with the liquid. Return the pan to the freezer and continue to freeze, stirring periodically for 3 hours, until all the liquid is frozen and the crystals are small flakes. Spoon the granita into chilled goblets and garnish each with a lemon twist. Serve immediately.

PER SERVING

Calories 7

Protein .12 grams

Carbohydrate 1.6 grams

Fiber 0 grams

Fat 0 grams

Net Carbs .8 grams

Chocolate Granita Espresso

This coffee "ice granulars" little grains of flavor (hence granita *in Italian) now becomes a chocolate treat that is light and refreshing.*

16   ounces fresh brewed espresso
¼   cup Splenda Granular
1   1-ounce square unsweetened baker's
       chocolate, grated
1   cup sweetened whipped cream

SERVES 4

While the espresso is still hot, add the Splenda and stir until dissolved. Chill thoroughly. Add grated chocolate. Pour the sweetened coffee into a shallow 9-inch pan to a depth of less than 1 inch. Put the pan in the freezer for 1 hour. Gently stir the ice crystals to mix with the liquid. Return the pan to the freezer and continue to freeze, stirring periodically for 3 hours, until all the liquid is frozen and the crystals are small flakes. Spoon the granita into chilled goblets and add whipped cream. Serve immediately.

PER SERVING

Calories 92	Protein 1.2 grams	Carbohydrate 7.2 grams
Fiber 1.1 grams	Fat 7.5 grams	Net Carbs 5 grams

Fresh Fruit Tart

This fruit tart was developed with you in mind. We want it,
we need it, I crave it—besides, we love sweets.

1   cup half-and-half
2   teaspoons grated lemon zest
3   tablespoons Splenda Granular, divided
3   egg yolks
1   tablespoon soy flour
2   teaspoons cornstarch
     Pinch of salt
1   cup whipped heavy cream, chilled
3   tablespoons butter, melted
2   sheets phyllo, thawed according to package directions
1½   tablespoons finely chopped toasted hazelnuts
1   cup chopped cherries or seedless grapes

YIELDS 16

Heat the half-and-half and lemon zest in a small saucepan to scalding, then turn the heat down very low for 5 minutes. Turn the heat off and steep until the half-and-half is infused with lemon flavor. Strain the half-and-half and discard the zest. Whisk 2 tablespoons of Splenda into the half-and-half until dissolved, and set aside.

Prepare a medium-sized bowl of ice water and set aside. In a small bowl, whisk the remaining tablespoon of Splenda with the egg yolks, flour, cornstarch, and salt. Whisk a little of the warm cream into the egg yolk mixture, then gradually add the rest of the cream. Pour the entire mixture into the saucepan; stirring constantly, cook over moderately low heat until thickened, about 5 minutes. Remove the pan from the heat and set it in the ice bath. Stir occasionally until cool, then set a piece of plastic directly on the surface to prevent a skin from forming. Chill thoroughly. When chilled, stir ⅓ of the whipped cream into the pastry cream, then fold in the rest and refrigerate.

Preheat the oven to 375°F. Cover a cookie sheet with parchment. Invert 16 mini baking cups on the cookie sheet and brush well with butter (repeat process if you have smaller amount of mini cups). Cut 2 sheets of 12-inch by 17-inch phyllo on top of each other. Cut them in half again, then again, and once more to a total of 32 pieces—2 pieces will be used on each cup.

Place one phyllo square on the work surface, keeping the remaining squares covered with a towel. Brush the square with butter, sprinkle with some of the hazelnuts and cover with a second sheet, in the opposite direction. Butter the sheet and shape it gently over the mini-cup, buttered-side down. Butter the outside of the shell. Repeat with the remaining shells. Bake for 8 to 10 minutes or until golden brown. Cool on a rack until cool enough to handle, then slide the shell off the cup and continue cooling on the rack.

Just before serving, divide the pastry cream among the mini phyllo shells, sprinkle with nuts, top with fruit, and serve immediately.

NOTE: You can buy prebaked small phyllo cups, but the carb count is 5 grams per 2 cups empty. Our cups have only 1.16 grams of carbs each.

PER SERVING

Calories 98	Protein 1.7 grams	Carbohydrate 4.4 grams
Fiber .39 grams	Fat 8 grams	Net Carbs 3.8 grams

Egg Custard

*This Italian dessert, zabaione in Italian, is from the Piedmont region.
It's very rich, so small servings are suggested.*

5   large egg yolks
5   tablespoons Splenda Granular
1   teaspoon grated orange zest
½   cup sweet Marsala

SERVES 4

Beat the egg yolks, Splenda, and orange zest together in the top of a
double boiler and set over simmering water. Use a whisk and continue to beat, gradually adding the Marsala.

Continue to beat until the mixture becomes foamy and thick.
Serve warm or chilled.

Variation: Sweeten and beat 1 cup of heavy cream (or use ready-made
dessert topping) and fold into the completed *zabaione*. Refrigerate for
a few hours or freeze for 20 to 30 minutes before serving.

PER SERVING

Calories 127   Protein 3.5 grams   Carbohydrate 5.9 grams
Fiber .05 grams   Fat 6.4 grams   Net Carbs 4.4 grams

Mom's Cheesecake

*I've made this cheesecake for years, but I must say that now,
Splenda Granular makes it even better.*

6   large egg whites
1½ pounds whole milk ricotta cheese
3   large egg yolks
1   cup Splenda Granular
    Juice of ½ orange
1½ tablespoons vanilla extract
1   tablespoon anisette liqueur
1   teaspoon orange zest
1   teaspoon baking powder
1   tablespoon confectioners' sugar for sprinkling

SERVES 10

Preheat the oven to 350°F.

In a large bowl, beat the egg whites until stiff and set aside.

In a separate large bowl, mix the ricotta cheese with the egg yolks,
Splenda, orange juice, vanilla, anisette, orange zest, and baking powder. Fold in the egg whites.

Pour into a greased and floured 8-inch springform pan. Bake for
1 to 1¼ hours or until done. Check with a cake tester or toothpick
inserted in the center of the cake. The tester should come out clean.
When cooking, a little liquid may ooze out; *this is normal.* Remove
from springform pan. Refrigerate when cool. Sprinkle with confectioners' sugar before serving.

PER SERVING

Calories 172	Protein 10.7 grams	Carbohydrate 7 grams
Fiber .03 grams	Fat 10.4 grams	Net Carbs 5.2 grams

Baked Pudding

BONET

If you have been good and you're rewarding yourself, then oh, this is the one!
It's called Bonet *in Italy and is from the Piedmont region. You owe me.*

6	tablespoons water, divided
4	tablespoons Splenda Granular, divided
1	tablespoon sugar
1½	cups heavy cream,
	plus ½–1 cup whipped cream for garnish
½	cup sugar-free amaretti cookies, crumbled
¼	cup strong espresso
¼	cup liqueur such as dark rum,
	coffee liqueur, or brandy
¼	cup unsweetened cocoa
4	eggs

SERVES 4

Preheat the oven to 300°F and prepare a hot water bath.

In a small saucepan, heat 3 tablespoons of the water with 2 tablespoons of Splenda and the sugar over medium heat, stirring occasionally, until the sugar dissolves. Increase the heat to high and, without stirring, cook the mixture until deep caramel colored, about 5 minutes. Remove from heat and slowly stir in the remaining water. Cool 5 minutes and divide among four 6-ounce to 8-ounce ramekins, and set aside.

In a small saucepan, heat the cream; add the cookie crumbles and set aside.

Whisk the espresso, liqueur, cocoa, 2 tablespoons of Splenda, and eggs together in a medium bowl. Gradually, whisk the cream mixture into the egg mixture, then strain the custard through a sieve into the ramekins. Put the ramekins in the water bath and bake 30 minutes or until set. Cool to room temperature and chill.

When ready to serve, set the ramekins in hot water for 10 seconds and invert onto a dessert plate. Serve with dollops of whipped cream.

PER SERVING

Calories 587	Protein 10.6 grams	Carbohydrate 21.5 grams
Fiber 2.4 grams	Fat 50 grams	Net Carbs 18 grams

Goat Cheese and Cherry Ramekins

Watch out when you eat these little treasures, because they have been known to cause people to book a trip to Italy.

4	ounces goat cheese
4	ounces mascarpone cheese
2	tablespoons Splenda Granular
2	eggs, beaten
¼	teaspoon vanilla extract
2	tablespoons fresh lemon juice, divided
¼	teaspoon lemon zest
½	pound fresh cherries, pitted and quartered
2	tablespoons water

SERVES 4

Combine the goat cheese and mascarpone in the bowl of a mixer and beat until smooth. Add the Splenda, eggs, vanilla, 1 tablespoon of lemon juice, and the zest and mix until smooth. Divide the mixture evenly among four ½-cup ramekins and cover each with a piece of foil. Put ramekins in a pan with hot water reaching halfway up sides of ramekins, and bake for 40 minutes. Ramekins are done when a sharp knife inserted into the middle comes out clean. Cool on rack to room temperature, cover, and chill.

In a small saucepan, bring cherries, water, and remaining lemon juice to a boil. Reduce heat to medium and cook until the liquid turns to syrup. Cool to room temperature before topping ramekins and serving.

PER SERVING

Calories 287	Protein 11.1 grams	Carbohydrate 12 grams
Fiber 1.4 grams	Fat 22 grams	Net Carbs 10 grams

Almond Ricotta

*I always enjoy showing how sometimes the simplest (and most delicious)
ingredients create wonders—you be the judge.*

¾ cup Splenda Granular
1 1-ounce square unsweetened
    baker's chocolate, grated
15 ounces whole milk ricotta cheese
2 tablespoons Amaretto liqueur,
    plus more for drizzling
1 cup fresh strawberries, sliced
⅓ cup sliced almonds, toasted *(see page 28)*

SERVES 4

Combine the Splenda and chocolate, then blend in ricotta cheese and
the 2 tablespoons of Amaretto.

Divide the sliced strawberries on 4 plates, drizzle with Amaretto,
and spoon on ricotta cheese mixture in a mound. Sprinkle with
almonds and serve.

PER SERVING

Calories 323	Protein 14.5 grams	Carbohydrate 16.9 grams
Fiber 2.7 grams	Fat 21.8 grams	Net Carbs 10.8 grams